STEVEN FURTICK

NEW YORK TIMES BEST-SELLING AUTHOR

(UN)QUALIFIED

HOW GOD USES BROKEN PEOPLE TO DO BIG THINGS

(UN)QUALIFIED

Italics in Scripture quotations reflect the author's added emphasis.

Details in some anecdotes and stories have been changed to protect the identities of the persons involved.

Trade Paperback ISBN 978-1-60142-460-0
Hardcover ISBN 978-1-60142-459-4
eBook ISBN 978-1-60142-461-7

Cover design by Ryan Hollingsworth; cover image of stained glass window by Henry Willet of Willet Hauser Architectural Glass Inc.

Published in association with the literary agency of Fedd and Company, Inc., P.O. Box 341973, Austin, TX 78734.

Published in the United States by Multnomah, an imprint of the Crown Publishing Group, a division of Penguin Random House LLC, New York.

MULTNOMAH® and its mountain colophon are registered trademarks of Penguin Random House LLC.

The Library of Congress has cataloged the hardcover edition as follows:
Names: Furtick, Steven.
Title: (Un)qualified : how God uses broken people to do big things / Steven Furtick.
Other titles: Unqualified
Description: First Edition. | Colorado Springs, Colorado : Multnomah Books, 2016. | Includes bibliographical references.
Identifiers: LCCN 2015033265 | ISBN 9781601424594 | ISBN 9781601424617 (electronic)
Subjects: LCSH: Self-actualization (Psychology)—Religious aspects—Christianity. | Failure (Psychology)—Religious aspects—Christianity. | Success—Religious aspects—Christianity.
Classification: LCC BV4598.2.F87 2016 | DDC 248.4—dc23
LC record available at http://lccn.loc.gov/2015033265

Printed in the United States of America
2019

10 9 8 7 6 5 4 3

I dedicate this book to Max.

You are the better man.

CONTENTS

There is a crack in everything.
That's how the light gets in.

Leonard Cohen

Unqualified

"What comes to your mind when you hear the name Steven Furtick?" the interviewer asked the renowned theologian.

Hey, they're talking about me!

I sprinted back into the room where the video was playing, secretly excited to be the center of attention. I had read this guy's book about ministry in seminary, so I was rather flattered he knew my name. We had never even met.

I had found this particular interview the way you discover most YouTube videos—by free-falling into the abyss that is the "recommended for you" sidebar. After I'd clicked it, I'd walked away to get dressed for church. I could still hear the interview in the background, but I wasn't really listening.

Until, out of nowhere, I heard that sweetest sound of all: my own name. It's always great to be recognized.

Except when it's not.

"What comes to your mind when you hear the name Steven Furtick?"

The theologian sighed and dropped his head, signifying that

the mere consideration of my name was wearisome. That got the crowd chuckling. Apparently they knew he wasn't a fan.

Long, pained pause. Agonized grimace. Bone-chilling stare.

Then the verdict.

"Unqualified."

He delivered the four syllables with a disgust that underscored the gravity and finality of his pronouncement. Only the gavel sound effect was missing.

No elaboration. No explanation. No qualifiers. My whole life and ministry summed up with a single word.

And abruptly the interview moved on.

Unqualified?

That word started the wheels spinning in my head. It was strange because part of me wanted to come to my defense (against YouTube?), but the other part was thinking, *Friend, you don't know the half of it.*

Yes, I struggle—with my temper, with my focus, with my motives, with my eating habits, with my prayer life, with my state of mind. And that list doesn't even scratch the surface.

I know my weaknesses and faults better than anyone. I don't need to listen to an online interview to feel disqualified. Hardly a day goes by that I'm not seized by the sensation that I have no business doing what I'm doing. That I'm in over my head. That I don't deserve any of my blessings or opportunities.

Am I unqualified?

This book is the answer to that question. I'm not writing it in reaction to that random interview on YouTube. I've been asking myself that question my whole life. And maybe you have too.

When I started the journey that lies behind this book, I wanted to finally figure out how to respond to that question within myself. I wanted to know if that theologian was correct. If the whispers of doubt that regularly rattle through my head are inner demons to be ignored—or warning bells to be heeded. If I should shoulder my responsibilities with confidence in my calling—or panic and hide before I mess everything up.

At one point or another, you've probably felt unqualified. Maybe you didn't have the dubious privilege of being informed of the fact via YouTube, but you knew it was true nonetheless.

I think we all secretly fight feelings of inadequacy, insufficiency, and incompetence. We wonder whether we really measure up. We fear we are not "enough"—whatever that means in our particular situations.

Maybe it's in your character. There is a flaw, a crack, a deficiency that you try your hardest to hide. It could be lust. It could be anger. It could be addiction. Even if it's in the past, you may live in secret fear that one day it will come back in fury and destroy everything you are building.

Maybe it's in your role as a parent. At the workplace you have everything under control. You can buy and sell and trade with the best of them. But your home life is another story. You have no idea how to raise your teenager, and you are feeling dangerously unprepared.

Or maybe you know something deep in your soul is propelling you into ministry. Not necessarily full-time but definitely something significant. You are supposed to be a leader, a decision maker, a risktaker. But your track record is far from spotless. And the thought of putting yourself out there is petrifying. What if you fail? And what if your failures shipwreck others along the way?

Many people live their entire lives fighting these contradictions. They deal constantly with voices in their heads telling them that they don't qualify, that they will never qualify, that they are totally, epically *disqualified.*

I wrote a book called *Crash the Chatterbox* about how to sort through negative thoughts. But this book isn't about just changing what rattles around in our minds or what comes out of our mouths. It's about understanding who we really are *now* in order to be who we are capable of *becoming.* It's about ruthlessly peeling back the prejudices and assumptions we've made about ourselves. It's about letting God be our source of sufficiency.

I have good news. If you look at the great men and women of Scripture, you find one common denominator: they were *all* unqualified. God has a habit of picking people who have been passed over.

Pass or Fail

Have you ever thought about who—or what—truly has the ability to qualify you? Who has the ultimate right to determine if you are a success or a failure?

It's not as simple as it sounds.

For example, think about the first qualification system most of us experience in life: grades. Schools invest huge amounts of money and manpower into developing standards and tests. They attempt to summarize students' academic progress with a universal system of numbers or letters.

Maybe you've been out of school for a while, but do you remember when your universe revolved around grades? Or maybe it didn't but your parents thought it should, in which case report-card day was probably terrifying. It was basically a preview of Judgment Day minus the cherubs and big white throne.

How did you feel when you got a passing grade? Probably relieved. Your parents were happy. Life was good again.

But think about it. Did that grade mean you learned the material? Or just that you were good at taking tests—or maybe cheating on them? Even more important, did your grade mean you actually knew how to apply what you had learned?

Or maybe you got a failing grade. Did that mean you would fail in life? Did the fact that you dated the American Revolution before Columbus or forgot the quadratic equation or thought the periodic table had something to do with punctuation really doom you to an inferior existence?

Most of us have been around long enough to know that that little letter or number is important, but it's not the final word. Not even close. History is filled with successful academic dropouts, from Abraham Lincoln to Walt Disney to Bill Gates.

This whole business of judging and assessing and qualifying one another doesn't stop with school. It is deeply ingrained in our culture and psyche. Just look at our clichés.

Pass the test.

Make the cut.

Fall short.

Measure up.

Make the grade.

Earn your stripes.

Pay your dues.

We constantly analyze and summarize each other. We compare people to our standards—spoken or unspoken—to see how they measure up. Then we accept them or reject them; we praise them or criticize them; we revere them or ridicule them. We all secretly administer exams in the university of our own opinions.

But just like grades in school, our evaluations don't usually tell the whole story. They are artificial, limited attempts to quantify something that can't really be reduced to a number, a letter, or a word.

But we keep trying. Because we're human, and that's what we do.

Basically, we tend to qualify people based on *character* and *competency.*

Character refers to who we are. Not just our names or nationalities, but our personalities, our morals, our values, our emotional makeup, our likes and dislikes, our tastes, our manners—the list goes on.

Competency refers to what we do. It's the complex sum of our training, achievements, talents, activities, and potential. It's about how good we are at what we do and about how much we accomplish.

Our competency is usually much more at the forefront than our character. What we *do* makes headlines. It fills the pages of our résumés. It is so intricately connected to our identity that we often think it *is* our identity.

Sooner or later, though, our character gets the last laugh. People might hire us and use us for what we do, but they accept us and like us for who we are. And ultimately, of course, who we are determines what we do. You can pretend for only so long before the real you comes out.

The moment we meet a new person, we size up that person. We don't do this consciously for the most part. And it isn't necessarily meanspirited. We automatically gather clues about the other person's character and competency. We start to categorize the person in relationship to us.

Will we be friends? Am I interested in knowing this individual better, or should we just be casual acquaintances? Will he advance my career? Does she need my help? Is he a threat to me? Does she have something to offer me, or do I have something to offer her?

It would be easy to lament how selfish all this sounds and to make the case that our standards for others are so subjective and hypocritical they are laughable.

But I don't think that would really do humankind justice. Of course there are elements of subjectivity and self-centeredness in our relationships with others. That is part of life in a broken, fallen world. It is an instinct for self-preservation.

It's not realistic to expect people to accept each other at face value. Nor is it healthy to be naive and assume that everyone is our best friend or has our best interest at heart. That's why Jesus told us to be wise as serpents and harmless as doves.

But here's a point worth noting. We tend to be exceptionally poor judges of other people. Have you noticed? And frankly we aren't even that good at judging ourselves.

That lack of accuracy, more than our tendency to assess others in the first place, is the problem.

I think that's what seemed kind of outrageous about the comments from my YouTube critic. Where did this guy get his information? His standards? His authority?

I'm not trying to judge his judgmentalism. That would be ironic. But I do have to decide how to react to it. And I don't mean my public response.

I'm talking about something far more important: my internal response. How do I view myself? How do I react to the criticism and assessments of a world obsessed with qualifications? How do I silence my own doubts, insecurities, and fears of failure?

The answer isn't what you would think. Or at least it wasn't what I thought when I started this journey.

The Qualification Trap

I used to think that the answer to my failures was to fix them, that the solution to my weaknesses was to replace them with strengths. I assumed the secret to success was to appear as perfect, flawless, and superhuman as possible. I concluded that my character and my competency qualified me or disqualified me.

But God's qualification system is much different from ours. And so is his way of approaching our weaknesses. Rather than stressing and obsessing over our lack, we need to find a different qualifier.

In the next few chapters, we are going to explore what it means to be qualified God's way. I believe it will revolutionize the way you see yourself and others. That's what it has done for me.

As you understand how God sees you, you will find the freedom and self-confidence that he wants for your life.

You will never get those things from human qualifications, by the way. That's a dead-end street. You could never be perfect enough or failproof enough to be at peace with yourself on that basis alone.

Peace and confidence come through one thing: acceptance. In a culture fixated on self-improvement and self-help, that might seem counterintuitive. But it's true.

First, *God's unconditional acceptance of you.* God knows your true identity—the real you—and he loves you just as you are.

Second, *your acceptance of yourself, including your weaknesses.* That means confronting the parts of you that you may prefer to ignore. And it means knowing who you are (and who you are not) in and through Jesus.

And third, *your acceptance of God's process of change.* God's work in your life isn't meant to squelch or eradicate the real you but rather to bring out the best possible version of you.

Those three concepts—identity, weakness, and change—will show up again and again in this book because they are directly related to this issue of being qualified.

The three have a cyclical relationship. I know the "real me"—my identity—all too well. I know I have many weaknesses. That makes me feel unqualified, so I try to change my weaknesses. But reality soon sinks in. I can't completely fix myself. So my identity suffers even more, and I feel even less qualified.

As long as my answer to my lack of qualifications is just to try harder to qualify myself, I'll stay stuck in that cycle.

Has that ever happened to you? Do your failures ever shout so loudly you can't hear the opportunities? Do your self-doubts ever sabotage your success before you even get out of the gate?

The gap between who you are and what you want to accomplish can feel impossibly wide, and the question is left looming: *Am I qualified for this?*

Now let me say this up-front—that question is not the problem. You *should* ask yourself if you are qualified. Especially if you are trying to fly an airplane or perform open-heart surgery. In those cases, by all means, evaluate your training, your knowledge, your experience, and your abilities. We will all thank you for it. And certainly there are ethical and moral standards to uphold not only in ministry but in any field.

But when it comes to more subjective matters, keep in mind that your assessment is not infallible. And maybe, just maybe, you are overestimating your shortcomings and underestimating your gifts. Maybe the fact that you don't currently measure up to the expectations you or other people have isn't a deal killer. Maybe God wants to do something beyond your abilities, and he is far less intimidated by your failures and limits than you are.

The more I study these subjects in the Bible, the more convinced I am that we need a fuller understanding of ourselves and of God. And we need to give less weight to our opinion of our weaknesses and problems.

The feeling of being unqualified produces all kinds of bizarre behavior. We pretend to have everything together when really it's falling apart. Or we think everything is falling apart just when it's on the verge of coming together. We live under a constant cloud of comparison. We manipulate and scheme because we think trickery is the only way to get what we want.

Insecurity, comparison, manipulation, pretense—they all come from a wrong understanding of what it means to be approved and qualified by God.

But God's solution to our shortcomings is not necessarily to fix them. He has a better idea, as we'll see in the following pages.

Paradoxical Patriarch

One of the most dramatically unqualified biblical heroes I can think of is Jacob. Awhile back I was studying the life of this man in preparation for a sermon series. Out of nowhere a thought rattled me.

God can't bless who you pretend to be.

Prior to that thought I was wondering why in the world I had chosen to preach about this paradoxical patriarch for the next five weeks. He was turning out to be the most complicated biblical antihero I'd ever studied. Most of the stories involving Jacob are like episodes of *The Sopranos*—you don't know whom to root for because everyone is messed up. Like the time Jacob's uncle tricked him into getting drunk and accidentally sleeping with the wrong woman on his wedding night.

Jacob was a liar, a con, a trickster, a fraud. He spent much of his life haunted by bad decisions and exiled to the chaos of self-inflicted consequences. If anyone deserved to be called unqualified, it was this guy. He was not exactly the character that neat sermon outlines and Sunday school lessons are made of.

And yet God called him. Chose him. Even blessed him. And Jacob ended up playing a major role in God's plan to redeem the world. He emerges as simultaneously one of the most important figures in Scripture and one of the most screwed up.

That Thursday afternoon with my Bible open and my notes out, I was blindsided by the realization that I am just like Jacob in so many ways. Not nearly as important in the scheme of human history, of course. But every bit as unqualified from a human perspective. And every bit as valuable and loved in God's eyes.

Just like Jacob I often find myself pretending to be someone I'm not because I'm embarrassed about who I am. I think my weaknesses are the problem and faking it till I make it is the solution.

But God can't bless someone I'm not. He longs to bless me. The real *me,* with all my ups and downs and pros and cons.

The more I analyzed the story of Jacob, the more I saw God as the Qualifier. Jacob was a poster child for the confusion and complications that weaknesses produce. But he was also a dramatic example of someone who was, at least by the end of his life, able to embrace his insufficiencies, look past them, and trust in God.

And when he did, God took over. He overruled Jacob's limitations and trumped his disqualifications.

Jacob was acutely, painfully, spectacularly human. That's probably why his life speaks so clearly to me. I can relate to his failures faster than his feats, and I bet you can too.

What I learned through studying Jacob radically shifted my

thinking. In the last few chapters of this book, I'll address Jacob's life in more detail. His story gives us a fascinating case study in God's power at work in our weaknesses.

Ultimately God redeemed, redefined, and realigned Jacob not in spite of but through his weaknesses. And that's what he will do for you and me.

On the day the theologian informed me of my utter unqualifiedness, God reminded me of a verse that talks about our qualifications: "It is not that we think we are qualified to do anything on our own. Our qualification comes from God. He has enabled us to be ministers of his new covenant" (2 Corinthians 3:5–6, NLT).

All of a sudden I felt liberated.

Yes, *unqualified* suits me just fine. It has a nice ring to it. And it puts me in some pretty good company, starting with Jacob.

So go ahead and put it on my business card. And in my Twitter bio too.

God called me. *God* equipped me. *God* empowered me. *God* opened doors for me. So my qualifications, or lack thereof, were relatively irrelevant.

Yes, I had some ground to stand on if I wanted to defend my ministerial pedigree. But why? It's the truth: God has blessed my efforts far beyond what I could ever deserve. And that's amazing! Really, why would I want to limit my influence and success merely to what I qualify for?

"Unqualified" wasn't a criticism. It was a compliment. Granted, an unintended, backhanded compliment, but a compliment nonetheless. It was a public reminder that God has done so much more than I deserve in and through me.

I hope that doesn't sound proud, because it's not. I think it's actually the opposite of pride. Humility—true humility—isn't putting yourself down. It's recognizing that you owe everything to God. It's stepping into your destiny based not on who you are or what you can do but on who God is and what he will do through you.

I'm sure that theologian loves God and the church. When we both get to heaven someday, perhaps I'll invite him over to my place for some boiled peanuts, and maybe we'll laugh about the whole thing.

But right now what matters most isn't what comes to another person's mind when he hears my name. What matters most is what comes to *God's* mind and *my* mind.

I ended up watching that little part of the interview five more times. I was laughing out loud by the last time. I texted the link to a few friends. I briefly considered how funny it would be to make it into a meme for Instagram.

Then I finished getting ready for church. Before the service I prayed with my team as I do almost every weekend. As we were closing the prayer, I added an unusual line. My team probably wondered what in the world I was talking about, but it made me smile, and it filled me with a strange confidence and gratitude.

"And thank you, Lord, . . . that we are unqualified."

THE THIRD WORD

"I am Steven."

I've said it thousands of times. I've spelled it almost as many, because if you don't alert people to the *v* they'll stick a *ph* in the middle every time.

And don't get me started on *Furtick*.

What is the key word in the phrase *I am Steven*? It's the name, right? *Steven*. That's what identifies me. The first two words—*I am*—are just there to set up the statement. They are filler. Just insignificant monosyllabic fluff.

Or are they?

Hold that thought.

2

The Name Game

I have a phobia. It's a strange one, I admit.

I'm scared to ask people who are expecting a child what they're planning to name their offspring. Why? Because lately it seems as if people name their children—how do I say this?—creatively.

It's their right to name their child whatever they want. I understand that. But the reason I don't ask is because I'm not good at faking my reaction.

If I say, "What are you going to name him?" and they say something that is going to get the kid beat up in junior high, I'm likely to respond with a stunned "huh," which is typically not the response they're looking for. So I no longer ask the question. It's just too much liability. It's better to find out in private, where I can react without hurting their feelings.

For the record my first name is not Steven. My first name is Larry. My actual name is Larry Stevens Furtick Jr. The reason it's *Stevens* is because my father's middle name was misspelled on his birth certificate. Rather than changing his name, he transferred the mistake to my birth certificate. Thanks, Dad.

It could have been worse. What my dad originally wanted to name me still makes me shudder.

My father wanted to name me Clem. You see, my mom graduated from Clemson University in South Carolina. So my dad thought it would be a real trip if, when he called me, he could say, "Clem! Son! Come here, Clem, Son."

Thank God my mom intervened.

There are worse names than that, though. Recently one of my staff members told me about someone who named their child La–a.

He wrote it out for me, and I was confused about the proper pronunciation. You probably are too. If you think it should be pronounced "lah" or "lay," you are sadly mistaken.

It's pronounced "Luh-DASH-uh."

I don't have words to express the thoughts that went through my mind when I heard that one. I'm so sorry for you, La–a, wherever you are. We will be praying for you. Specifically, we will pray that when the angels write your name in the Lamb's Book of Life, they spell it right.

Luckily for the Clems and La–as of the world, while our given names identify us, they don't define us. They don't describe us. They don't say anything about who we really are, about our dreams, our feelings, our passions, or our potential.

I think most of us understand that our identities are much broader than our given names. But how much effort have we invested in really understanding what drives us and what we've allowed to define us?

When our perception of who we are is distorted, our entire

emotional equilibrium is off. That's why it hurts so much when we fail, when we fall short. Our shortcomings seem to prove that we are fundamentally flawed, and that makes us question our value and our identity.

As I said in the last chapter, God doesn't see things the way we do. His scales, his standards, and his measuring devices aren't calibrated the way ours are. But until we understand his way of thinking, we will look at our failures and successes as the sole indicators of our value. Inevitably that leads to exaggerated, constantly shifting conclusions about whether we are qualified or not.

An identity that is informed by feelings of inadequacy is a dangerous thing.

In the next few pages, I want us to get introspective about our identity. Perhaps more important, I want us to consider our *interpretation* of our identity. Do we know who we really are? Does this align with who God says we are? And what do we do about the space between?

That's complicated, because *we* are complicated. Thankfully, the Bible anticipates these complications.

What the Blank

Almost four thousand years ago, God called out from a burning bush to a man named Moses. The story is found in Exodus 3. If you've been around church for long, I'm sure you've heard some version of it. Here's the recap, laced with a few details from my imagination.

God found Moses in the middle of the desert and presented

a mind-blowing plan. He wanted Moses to march into Egypt, which happened to be the most powerful nation in the world at the time, and tell Pharaoh to release his work force of millions of Israelite slaves.

Moses's mind was blown, all right. But not in a good way. He started sweating and stuttering and hyperventilating at the mere prospect.

So Moses asked God what his name was. He was desperate to find something—anything—that could help convince the Israelites to buy into this scandalous scheme.

Instinctively Moses knew that God's identity was more important than anything else at that moment. More important than his own abilities or education or résumé. More important than the power of Pharaoh or the politics of Egypt or the practicality of becoming an instant abolitionist.

So God agreed to tell Moses his name.

"Moses, my name is . . . I AM."

Long, awkward pause. Moses leaned in, eagerly listening for the bush to give up its secrets. *Go on, I'm listening. You are . . . what? What are you? . . . Wait, that's the whole thing? Just "I AM"? What's the third word?*

But God didn't finish the sentence. For a perfect God, he seems to have some glaring grammar-usage problems. Doesn't he know that this verb takes a subject complement? That he needs to complete the thought?

Perhaps God was sending Moses—and each of us—a message: don't skip over the *I am.* Don't flippantly fill in the blank of who you are.

Think about those two words: *I am.* Such a tiny, underwhelming phrase. It's barely two syllables long.

Yet it is the most potent, revolutionary statement ever made. Within it is a power that can peel off the past, pilot the present, and frame the future.

I'm not being mystical or ethereal. This is intensely practical. God chose this phrase to describe himself precisely because identity and self-perception are foundational concepts in life. That's a huge component of God's *I AM* revelation to Moses.

Yet God's name doesn't need a third word, because God is everything and everyone and everywhere that he needs to be in every moment. He is the fullness, he is the completion, and he is the satisfaction of every need or desire we could ever know. You could string together every superlative and exaggeration and still not begin to describe God.

You and I need third words, though. We need to anchor our identities to specific, tangible, descriptive terms. We need to finish the sentence, and we do it all the time whether we realize it or not.

On the most generic macro level, that third word is your name.

But that is only the beginning.

The third word isn't just about the name your parents gave you or the nickname you've been stuck with since that one spring break. It's not about what you put on your nametag at a trade show or what your friends call you.

How would you complete the sentence "I am ______"? How would you fill in that blank? How would you describe yourself? It's not as easy as it sounds.

When you go to church, usually you're given a lot of handles on who God is. You'll hear about his love, holiness, justice, and goodness. We toss around theological terms like *omnipresence, omniscience,* and *omnipotence.* We learn to describe God in glorious detail, complete with scriptural footnotes. Of course, this is of supreme importance.

But often we don't know who *we* are. And that's a deadly disconnect.

See, it's one thing to know who *God* is to you, but who are you to you? Maybe you can describe and define God, but does that sync up with how you describe and define yourself?

It's not that we don't define ourselves. We do. We fill in the blank all the time. We just don't realize it. We don't stop to recognize the third words we use about ourselves. They are automatic, subconscious—and incredibly revealing. *I am a pretty good dad. I am a terrible home repairman. I am a remarkably aggressive driver. I am a mediocre musician. I am a success. I am a failure. I am . . .*

I'm calling it a third word, but obviously we fill in that blank with more than a single term. Our third word might be a phrase. It might be a list. It might be a fear or a feeling. It might be a memory or a trauma. It might be an accusation lodged deep in our psyche.

We've been filling in the blanks all our lives, but we seldom stop to question whether we've gotten our third words right.

I'm reminded of the fill-in-the-blank tests we all took in school. The teachers would replace one or two key words in a sentence with enigmatic lines, and we were supposed to figure out the words that belonged in the blanks.

That seems easy enough at first glance, but here's the problem. Each blank had one—and only one—correct answer. Either you got it right, or you got it wrong.

That's tough. At least with multiple-choice questions you had about a one-in-four chance of guessing correctly. And with essay questions you could bluff your way through and get some credit for your creativity, effort, and general malarkey. I'm good at general malarkey.

Not so with those unforgiving blanks. There was no room for error, no margin for mistakes. Filling in the blanks was all about knowing the correct answer.

Only one person had the right to decide what belonged in the blanks. It was the teacher. He or she passed ultimate judgment on what those spaces represented.

When it comes to your life, who has the right to fill in that blank? You? Your parents? Your friends? Your circumstances?

I recently watched an old *60 Minutes* interview with Bob Dylan. The interviewer asked why he changed his name from Robert Zimmerman to Bob Dylan.

"You call yourself what you want to call yourself," Dylan responded with his trademark nonchalance. "It's the land of the free."[1]

You can change your legal name easily enough. A Zimmerman can become a Dylan just by filling out the right forms. But what about the internal titles and names that define you? Who decides those? And what if you don't like how your blank has been filled in so far? Can the answer change? To what degree can it change? To what degree should it change?

And for that matter, is there really only one correct answer? Can all the nuances and complexities and contradictions of your life be summed up so succinctly?

These are real-life questions. They strike at the heart of our self-perception and sense of identity. You probably don't have to deal with the fill-in-the-blank questions of school anymore, but the *I am* questions of life are a much bigger challenge. You answer them every day. And your answers direct and redirect the course of your existence, for better and worse.

Here are some third words I hear all the time, from both my mouth and my mind: *Unqualified. Stupid. Strong. Driven. Screwed up. Loyal. Stuck. Hurting. Overwhelmed. Blessed. Capable. Disappointed. Broken. Hopeful. Jaded. Content.*

Which of those do you identify with? Circle them mentally. What word of your own would you write in? How often do you say or think that about yourself? Which word or words do you expect to circle a year from now? Ten years from now? Which ones will you teach your kids to circle?

Now, just for fun, change that word—the *third word.*

It changes everything.

Let's go a little further. How does your evaluation of yourself compare with who you've led others to believe that you are? How does it compare with who you would like to be? In other words are you pretending? Are you putting up a false front to cover up the deficiencies and weaknesses you see inside yourself?

A bigger question is how does all this compare with God's assessment of you? Your self-image, your self-description, your persona—does that line up with who you were created to be?

These are enormous questions. Confusing questions. Brave questions. Getting them right will take a lifetime.

But if you ignore them, you'll waste a lot of your life posing, pretending, posturing, performing, perfecting, pleasing, and proving. Yet you'll never find your real self.

Bleach It Like Beckham

Getting to know "your real self" can be complicated.

Years ago a hairstylist told me he wanted to give me the "Beckham look." The mere suggestion, however unrealistic, that I could even remotely resemble the great soccer god was flattering enough to get me in the door.

It was the first time I'd been to a professional for my hair-care needs in more than ten years. An old set of clippers from my dad's barbershop had always done the job for me. And I could handle my simple buzz cut all by myself in my garage.

But a Beckham look? On me? I was willing to pay top dollar for that.

Once I got in the chair, the agonizing process of bleaching my hair from its natural jet-black color to platinum blond almost made me regret my decision. Apparently I have a low pain tolerance, because I found myself wondering if other salons would have offered anesthesia.

When I emerged from my makeover, I wasn't exactly David Beckham. I wasn't exactly blond, either—more of a citrus orange. But the change was dramatic, and I got used to it.

I rocked the new color for a couple of years. Then one day I went back to black. One of the first people who saw it told me something that made me laugh out loud.

"I think you should change it back to blond" was this person's unsolicited advice. "On you, black just doesn't look very . . . natural."

Sometimes I wonder if our image and identity have been treated and retreated and bleached and burned so many times that the original color is beyond recognition. Even to ourselves.

Disillusionment gets layered upon disappointment, which gets layered upon failure, and our real selves end up buried so far down we don't remember who we actually are.

Filling in our third words gets complicated because our fractured past has turned us into walking contradictions. Are we who we *dream* of becoming? Or are we who we *act* like we are now?

On the one hand we still think big. We know God has built us for bigger and bolder things, and deep inside the calling still flickers.

There are days when our imagination runs wild with possibilities for the future and with our potential contributions to the world. We promise ourselves all kinds of things. We'll make more memories with the kids. We'll finish landscaping the yard. We'll spend more time volunteering at church. We'll clean out the closet, enroll in that class, work on our abs, sponsor an orphan, write a book, coach the baseball team, change the world . . .

But on the other hand, we've become more realistic—or more cynical. It's hard to tell sometimes.

Achieving our goals is tougher than we thought it would be. We've tried and failed and tried again . . . and failed again. Now we aren't sure we're capable of raising toddlers or navigating credit card debt, much less tackling world change.

Maybe our dreams were never meant to be. Or maybe we just aren't strong enough or brave enough or some other *enough* to achieve them.

Maybe we *are* unqualified.

Dual Dichotomies

I talk to people all the time who wrestle with the gap between their weaknesses and their dreams, between who they are and who God says they are meant to be. Their third words are a clear indication that they feel unqualified.

People like Jamar, who told me that he feels a calling to make a difference in the lives of young men. Jamar grew up without a dad. He had to learn a lot of things the hard way, and he dreams of sharing with other young men the perspective and leadership he never had. If only . . . he didn't struggle with sexual addiction.

He's single and good-looking with a great smile and success in his job. He's popular with the ladies, and he knows it.

For stretches of time he has great success living by God's standards. But then temptation gets the best of him. Sexual sin derails him. How can he be an example to others when he needs so much help himself?

Jamar is frustrated because he sees glimpses of his ideal self. But a root of dysfunction is poisoning his growth. And so he concludes, *I am . . . stuck.*

And people like Heather. Heather is an amazing mom. At

least everybody but Heather thinks she is. Her kids are thriving. They are in multiple after-school activities, both artistic and athletic. None of them is addicted to meth. That's always a positive. She cooks for her family several nights a week. She usually reads a chapter of a book to her children before bedtime.

But somehow it's never enough. After the kids are down, all she sees is the mess she didn't get around to straightening that day. All she remembers is how she lost her temper when she was helping with homework. How can she celebrate her success as a mom in the midst of her many messes and misses?

Her Pinterest board is pinned with enough good intentions to fill three lifetimes. She has started four one-year reading plans this year on her Bible app, and at the rate she's going, she may finish one in the next decade. She feels pulled and pushed by a never-ending list of priorities. A voice in her head whispers that there is no depth to anything she's doing, that she is mediocre, that life is leaving her behind. All of this has her convinced, *I am . . . failing.*

And people like my brother, Max. I love Max. But for a long time, I helped drive him away from God.

Max and I grew up in a good southern home. That meant we ate chicken and dumplings and went to church at least once a week. Max is three years younger and six inches taller than I am. Also his real name isn't Max; it's Matthew. Imposing nicknames on people is a bad habit of mine, and I started calling him Max around the time I turned sixteen.

Coincidentally, that was around the time I started getting serious about my faith in Jesus. Since I had decided to walk the straight and narrow, I was determined that everyone around me would come along whether they liked it or not.

That included Max. He was the first of my forced converts, and he bore the brunt of my newfound religious zeal.

When I drove him to school, he usually wanted to listen to 96 WAVE, the rock station. Not a chance. Not in my car. We listened to Christian rock.

When I dropped him off at school, sometimes I'd catch him checking out a girl. *Busted lusting,* I would think. And I would scold him as though he belonged in Sodom and Gomorrah.

At night I'd walk into the living room and find him watching *Beavis and Butt-Head.* I would quickly change the channel to the first preacher I could find.

I wasn't trying to be a judgmental jerk. I loved my brother. And since I loved him, I thought it was my responsibility to show him the way to Jesus, even if that meant dragging him into holiness.

But he didn't seem to be following. I couldn't understand why.

I didn't recognize until the night of my dad's death, sixteen years later, that I had actually pushed him in the opposite direction.

I remember that night clearly. By the time the friends who had gathered to support our family had left, it was one o'clock in the morning. It had been the longest week of our lives, and we needed to rest. Max settled into a recliner in our mom's living room, and I stretched out on the couch.

Suddenly, unexpectedly, Max started sharing about his inner

struggles during those years. About how he had wanted to have a relationship with God for a long time, but it seemed too hard.

"It's not meant to be hard," I told him.

"But that's the way it always looked to me," he explained. "I watched you in high school. You had all these rules, all these things you couldn't do or say or watch or listen to. And I didn't want to be a fake Christian. But if that's what it meant to be a real Christian, I knew I couldn't do it. It was just too hard."

We talked for a while, and I apologized to Max. I told him I was sorry for making it look like the starting point of a relationship with God was buying into a list of restrictions. I told him I had learned over time that the gospel isn't about what God wants *from* us but what he wants *for* us.

The conversation definitely sparked something. Not only in Max but in me. I couldn't stop thinking about the phrase he used: *too hard.* It haunted me.

Is that how I'm making it look? Too hard? Is that how it's supposed to look? Is that how it's supposed to be?

How many people have given up on the idea that they could have a relationship with God because of all the qualifications we've attached to what it means to know him?

In some ways faith is going to be hard. To quote the old country preacher, "Jesus said take up your cross, not your Tempur-Pedic mattress." I get that. Forging a real life with God in this world is a complicated and difficult endeavor at times. But making people feel as if there are fifteen prerequisite steps to approaching God can't be what he had in mind when he called his message "good news."

He placed this invitation near the end of the Bible: "The Spirit and the bride say, 'Come!' And let the one who hears say, 'Come!' Let the one who is thirsty come; and let the one who wishes take the free gift of the water of life" (Revelation 22:17).

God seems to be saying, "Come as you are." Too often the message we project is "Change who you are, and then you can come."

Instead of helping my brother find God, I had actually created a force field that was keeping him from God. I had unintentionally planted the seed of a third word in his soul that might be the most dangerous word of all: *I am . . . unworthy.*

What are your third words? Are they mostly negative or positive? Are they so tangled that you can't even categorize them?

If you are anything like Jamar and Heather and Max and me, your third words tend to revolve around your weaknesses. They probably have a lot to do with who you are *not,* with what you *can't* do, or with what you feel that you are *failing* at doing. And so, because your character has cracks and your competency is questionable, you tend to feel unqualified and inadequate.

That's just the way we think.

This is a no-brainer, but I'm going to say it anyway: we all have weaknesses. We call them all sorts of things: hang-ups, slip-ups, screw-ups, mistakes, problems, sins, errors, faults, inner demons, addictions. But we all have them.

And whether we like it or not, they have a lot to do with how we see ourselves and, therefore, how we live our lives.

The pivotal question is, what are we supposed to *do* about our weaknesses?

This book is the result of wrestling with that question and others like it that have bothered me for years. Questions about self-acceptance. Questions about self-improvement. Questions about who I am versus who I am meant to be and how to reconcile the two.

I have to admit, this hasn't been an easy book to write. It's not that the topic is particularly controversial. It's been hard to write because it's messy.

Like life. Like humanity. Like you and me.

If you've ever been frustrated by your failures or exasperated by your weaknesses, this book is for you. But let me warn you, I'm not going to tell you fifteen ways to fix yourself in fifteen minutes a day. I'm not going to give you ten principles of perfection or seven secrets to success.

I want to do something that is, I hope, a lot more valuable.

I want to be real.

Real about struggles. Real about sin. Real about who God is and about who we are and about who we aren't. Real about self-esteem and self-help and about how sometimes we can't seem to fix certain things . . . and maybe we aren't supposed to.

This is a book about finding and embracing who you are in light of who God is. It's a book about coming to terms with the good, the bad, and the unmentionable in your life and learning how to let God use your mess for your benefit.

It is not about ignoring your complexities or denying your challenges. Far from it. But it's not about wallowing in self-pity and defeat, either.

It's about charging into the gap between who you are and

who you sense you were meant to be and then connecting with God there. It's about pursuing the dreams and desires God put in your heart even when it feels as if ten thousand demons are dispatched to chase you away.

As I've wrestled with my own questions on this topic, I've found myself changing. I've learned some things about weakness that I never understood before. I've come to see God and myself differently, and it's changing the way I parent, the way I pastor, and the way I approach God and life. And I love the changes.

So here is my question . . . or actually questions.

First, what are *your* third words?

Second, and more important, what are *God's* third words for your life?

And third, and most important of all, how in the world do you live right now, caught in the dichotomy between dual realities?

You're about to find out.

3

It's Complicated

Anytime you're processing your soul's deepest questions, there's only one source that guarantees answers: the movie *Shrek*.

The title character is an ogre. But he's not your average, disgusting, one-dimensional brute.

He is complicated. He is conflicted. He is emotional. And that's why we love him. I like how Shrek describes himself to his incessantly verbal sidekick, Donkey, by comparing himself to an onion.

> SHREK: Onions have layers. Ogres have layers . . . You get it? We both have layers.

Then Donkey goes off on a tangent, discussing layers, cake, and parfait. A few scenes later we find Shrek in an outhouse. Donkey is outside, yelling at him.

> DONKEY: You're so wrapped up in layers, onion boy, you're afraid of your own feelings![2]

That's exactly where a lot of us are. Wrapped up in layers. Afraid of our feelings. And locked in outhouses.

Okay maybe not that last part.

The truth is, we are complicated creatures. Our identities are a convoluted mix of emotions, memories, thoughts, goals, habits, prejudices, and philosophies. We defy simple descriptions or definitions.

We have layers, all right. More layers than ogres, onions, cakes, and parfaits put together. That's part of the beauty of being human.

On top of that, we aren't static beings. We aren't finished products. We aren't Jackson Pollock paintings to be analyzed and admired and appraised. We are constantly morphing, continually reinventing ourselves.

So if you haven't figured yourself out yet, that's okay.

Fresco Fiasco

A lot of books out there attempt to classify and categorize the human race. They dissect our dispositions and parse our personalities. They look at how we think, how we lead, how we love. They try to quantify the murky influences of ethnicity, culture, background, experience, education, brain chemistry, trauma, age, sexuality, and more.

I appreciate those attempts. At least on a macro level, they give us insight into ourselves and those around us. They help us understand and relate to our spouses, children, coworkers, and friends.

But they all break down at some point, because humans are too complicated to fit into any organizational scheme.

Personally, I prefer it that way. I don't want to be labeled and lumped together with millions of people just like me—or even with dozens of people just like me. I have friends who can effortlessly recite the results of their personality tests. And they swear by them as the master grid that predicts 90 percent of all human behavior. I took the same test. I've taken a few of them, actually. I couldn't tell you my results if you had a gun to my head. Somehow that stuff doesn't register with me enough to remember. And when someone tries to explain it, all I hear is Charlie Brown's teacher.

But there is something within each of us that tells us we are unique. Special. Original. I want to be me, just like you.

That nebulous *something* comes from God. It's his way of urging destiny upon us. He formed us and fashioned us, one at a time. David famously wrote about our identities and destinies in Psalm 139, which we'll look at throughout this chapter.

> You made all the delicate, inner parts of my body
> and knit me together in my mother's womb.
> Thank you for making me so wonderfully complex!
> (verses 13–14, NLT)

In other words God made you complex on purpose. You are layered infinitely more intentionally and intricately than Beethoven's Fifth Symphony.

In the next few pages, we are going to talk a lot about who we are. We are going to look at how our weaknesses and strengths affect us and how they relate to whether or not we feel qualified.

But here's the danger. If we don't recognize the value that is intrinsic in our complexity, our attempts to fix what we think is damaged could end up backfiring.

A few years ago an amateur art restorer in Spain made headlines for doing just that. She didn't mean to, of course. She was just trying to help.

Her name was Cecilia Giménez,[3] an eighty-year-old parishioner at the Sanctuary of Mercy church in Borja, Spain.

In the early nineteen hundreds a local artist had painted a fresco of Jesus on the wall of the church. It was known as *Ecce Homo* ("Behold the Man"). The painting had great sentimental value for the church and town, but it was certainly worse for the wear. The paint had faded, cracked, and in places peeled off completely.

Enter Cecilia. In her words, "We saw that everything was falling down, and we fixed it."

Only she didn't fix it.

What she lacked in training and talent she tried to make up for in quantity of paint. The result is best described as monstrous. The "restored" fresco looks like a cross between Bigfoot and Attila the Hun. It is so bad it became an Internet meme. Instead of *Ecce Homo,* it is now called *Ecce Mono* ("Behold the Monkey").

So much for restoration.

But sometimes we do the same thing. In the name of fixing ourselves, we can end up making things worse.

We don't mean to. Any more than a misguided, overzealous octogenarian meant to turn a fresco into a fiasco.

We look at ourselves and make simplistic judgments about

what is good and what is bad. About what is right and what is wrong. About what should stay and what should go.

We take a cursory glance in the mirror, compare ourselves to some arbitrary idea of what we are supposed to look like, and then start slapping paint around.

However, if our frame of reference is off, our improvement efforts will lead to everything but.

Remember, God isn't in the business of bleaching and sandblasting our identities. God is a restorer. God is a creator and a re-creator. He brings out the subtle hues and the deep tones that are hidden under layers of grit and grime.

That takes time. Skill. Effort.

We are as priceless as we are complex. We are as valuable as we are unique. It wouldn't be just unrealistic to oversimplify our identities. It would be tragic. Before charging into some self-restoration project, we need to take a close look at who God made us to be.

But that's going to require honesty, humility, and diligence. It's going to mean listening closely to the One who created us in the first place.

God Only Knows

Really, only God is capable of completely knowing the human heart. Jeremiah wrote, "The heart is deceitful above all things and beyond cure. Who can understand it? 'I the Lord search the heart and examine the mind'" (Jeremiah 17:9–10).

David said this about God's knowledge of us: "You have

searched me, LORD, and you know me. You know when I sit and when I rise; you perceive my thoughts from afar" (Psalm 139:1–2).

God knows you better than you know yourself. He looks inside the deepest crevices of your heart. He sees the secrets you've hidden from everyone, maybe even yourself.

And here's the best part. God knows everything about you—including the ugly parts, the broken parts, and the dysfunctional parts—yet he still believes in you. He still has a future and a hope for you.

My wife, Holly, said something to me one day that I think perfectly sums up what God would say to each of us: "I love everything there is to know about you."

I'm not here to analyze you or criticize you. I'm not out to make judgments about who you are right now or who you should become.

That's your journey.

My hope is to help you get the most out of that journey. It's to suggest how you can get unstuck if somehow your third words are spinning you out. It's to encourage you to embrace, and maybe even appreciate, many of the quirks and flaws that often drive you crazy. And it's to cheer you on as you allow God to bring out the real you.

Whatever that looks like.

Our third words affect every facet of our lives, but many of us never take the time to let God help us figure out what they are, if they are correct, or if any are missing.

Often we think we know who we are supposed to be. We

have an image in our heads of the perfect version of ourselves. And we dedicate a lot of time, effort, and desperate prayers to manifesting or manufacturing that image.

But the more I walk with God and the more I see the unexpected ways he uses unlikely people, the more convinced I am that we often have an incomplete image of who we were meant to be.

Before we launch into some well-intentioned but amateur restoration attempt, we need God to reveal who we are and who we can become. Maybe some of the things we think are dirt and grime are actually essential parts of who we are. Maybe some areas we call weaknesses are really strengths in disguise. They bother us now, but God has plans to use them for our benefit. They are an essential part of who God made us to be. Erasing them would be a travesty.

On the other hand maybe some areas we wish we could improve aren't part of our true identities at all. We want them to be, because we've been listening to other people's misguided expectations or our own unhealthy comparisons. We feel frustrated because we can't make progress. But it is impossible to multiply what God didn't give you to begin with. We need to drop those pursuits and instead focus on what God has entrusted to us.

In a Word

I've noticed that many of us tend to put too much emphasis on one or two third words. Usually they are the negative ones. We get discouraged, distracted, and derailed by our pessimistic I ams, our gloomy self-perceptions, and our cynical self-definitions.

There might be some truth to what we think. But odds are, we are generalizing and oversimplifying, and it's hurting our sense of purpose. David wrote this in Psalm 139:

> You saw me before I was born.
> Every day of my life was recorded in your book.
> Every moment was laid out
> before a single day had passed.
>
> How precious are your thoughts about me, O God.
> They cannot be numbered!
> I can't even count them;
> they outnumber the grains of sand! (verses 16–18, NLT)

David says that God's thoughts about us are *precious.* That's comforting. I'm glad to know they aren't frustrating or exasperating, the way I feel about myself so much of the time. *Precious* is a good word. But David doesn't stop there.

God's thoughts are also *innumerable.* Think about that for a second. The psalmist says it three different ways in two tiny verses: they *cannot be numbered,* we *can't even count them,* and they *outnumber the grains of sand.*

What does that tell us? That God's thoughts about us are as complex as we are. He doesn't oversimplify us. He doesn't lump us into categories, label us with scientific-sounding names, and alphabetize us on shelves.

God knows us intricately and intimately. He sees our past, present, and future. Every moment of every day of our lives is laid out before him. He is more aware of our complexity than anyone, including ourselves. He designed us, he delights in us, and he understands us.

So if God doesn't sum us up in a single phrase, why do we think we should?

But we do it all the time. We look at ourselves in the metaphorical mirror, sigh in disgust, and pronounce things like this:

I am a failure.

I am an alcoholic.

I am dumb.

I am hopeless.

Really? With one line, with one word, we sum up our entire identity, existence, and potential? With such flippancy we dismiss our calling and stamp ourselves *unqualified*?

That's ridiculous. No one is that simple. We are living, moving, changing, growing beings. There are more dimensions to our existence than the most complicated theories of wormholes and alternate universes could ever postulate.

God himself refuses to reduce us to a single flat image. He doesn't merge all our layers and levels into a two-dimensional image. He doesn't sum us up in a word.

So why do we?

I'm not suggesting we stop using third words. They are part of life, and they can be tremendously liberating—when we get them right.

What I'm saying is that we need to avoid putting labels and lids on ourselves that are too broad. Too simplistic. Too shortsighted.

We need to give our complexity some credit. We have to

embrace the fact that our identities are beautiful, delicate, and complicated things. They are works of art, and God has a lot invested in them.

Are they a little worse for the wear? Probably. Could they use some restoration? Of course. But God is the restorer, and he is going to take his time to do the job right.

Layers upon Layers

So ask yourself, *Who am I?* Take a moment to think about that. You might even want to get out a piece of paper and brainstorm as many descriptors as you can think of.

The complexity of the answer might just surprise you.

Here are a few categories to get you thinking, along with a handful of examples under each one. I've included quite a few negative third words as examples, not because I'm channeling Eeyore or Edgar Allan Poe, but because those are the ones that tend to shout at us the loudest and affect us the most. Plus, the idea here isn't to list the things you wish you were or even the things you have the potential to be. The idea is to describe accurately what you see when you see yourself right now.

You have third words in every single category below, whether you've ever stopped to verbalize them or not. You have layers upon layers upon layers of identity.

I suggest looking at the categories and writing down at least one word in each. More than one in some cases. Write down the words that describe you or that you hear resonating in your mind regularly. It doesn't have to be an exhaustive list, but I want you to see how pervasive and how important your *I am* statements really are.

Personality

I am shy. I am loud. I am a people pleaser. I am driven . . .

Character

I am honest. I am lazy. I am mean. I am trustworthy. I am selfish . . .

Conditions/Circumstances

I am exhausted. I am healed. I am blessed. I am broke . . .

Ability

I am stupid. I am musical. I am athletic. I am weak . . .

Emotions

I am scared. I am conflicted. I am overwhelmed. I am hurting . . .

Physical Traits

I am slow. I am male. I am tall. I am out of shape . . .

Education

I am a dropout. I am a straight-A student. I am a college graduate . . .

Family

I am single. I am a parent. I am divorced. I am a widow . . .

Ethnicity/Culture

I am American. I am Caucasian. I am Hispanic. I am small town. I am big city . . .

Sexuality

I am straight. I am gay. I am lesbian. I am bisexual. I am unsure . . .

Occupation

I am an engineer. I am a homemaker. I am unemployed. I am an entrepreneur . . .

Spirituality

I am Catholic. I am an atheist. I am agnostic. I am Christian . . .

Are you starting to get the picture? You have layers, onion boy. And that's something to celebrate. But it's also something to understand. Why? Because most of the time third words and phrases have baggage. They have emotional and psychological implications that resonate throughout our lives.

Let me give you a couple of examples. Look at two of the more external categories we just listed: ethnicity and occupation. Both are easy to identify and label. Anyone can look at our lives, even from the outside, and probably figure those out. And they are both amoral; that is, neither is positive or negative in itself.

Now ask yourself, what if they were different? How would that affect the way I think, act, and view myself?

I happen to be American. What would my life be like if I had been born in a different country? Again, it wouldn't necessarily be better or worse, but it would be profoundly different. Actually, I can hardly imagine it. It would affect me to my core. Language, culture, habits, customs, geography, my disdain for soccer—my identity is deeply rooted in my ethnicity.

Same goes for my occupation. I am a pastor and an author.

That colors and complicates my life in ways I rarely stop to consider. What would my life look like if I were, say, a plumber? That would never happen, because I am home-improvement challenged, to put it mildly. Even after thirteen years of marriage, I still don't own a tool kit. But just for the sake of illustration, if by some glitch in the universe I were a plumber instead of a pastor, it would change everything, from those I spend time with to what clothes I wear to how often I go to Home Depot.

Keep in mind that ethnicity and occupation are relatively simple, objective third words. What about the rest of the list? What about the internal things? What about my emotional identity or my spiritual identity? What about my personality traits or my character traits?

What if I were an introvert or an extrovert? What if I were bitter or insecure or hurt? What if I were free or self-confident or empowered?

And which comes first—the label or the lifestyle? The chicken or the egg? Doesn't behavior follow being?

Again, the goal here isn't to psychoanalyze yourself or dissect every layer of your identity. But I do want you to see how inclusive, extensive, and significant your *I am* statements—your third words—are in your life.

Some of our third words are accurate, of course. But many are not. I can't state strongly enough how important it is to process those third words and deal with our strengths and weaknesses correctly. For better or for worse, your third words direct your existence. You have a great deal of control over them, but in order to control them, you must first recognize them.

That's not easy, but it's not impossible, either. The real you is not an indecipherable, unknowable enigma. We already saw that God knows our identities perfectly. And I believe he wants to help us know ourselves as well.

Psalm 139 ends by saying precisely that.

> Search me, God, and know my heart;
>   test me and know my anxious thoughts.
> See if there is any offensive way in me,
>   and lead me in the way everlasting. (verses 23–24)

David asks God to *know* him, to *test* him, and to *lead* him.

That's exactly the attitude we need to take.

Admit we don't have all the answers. Recognize that God does. And commit to the process.

Yes, we are complicated. We'll never understand every thread, knot, and tangle in the tapestry of our identity. But the more you grow to know God, the more you will grow to know and, I believe, enjoy yourself.

I can't promise that the journey of self-discovery will be easy. You might have a few closets to clean out. There might be some secrets hidden under the floorboards. But if you can learn to recognize and value the real you, you'll find freedom and peace unlike anything you've ever experienced.

So who are you? Really?

4

Keeping It Real

I love music. I always have. And I guess I've always enjoyed being on stage in front of people. I'm sure a good personality test could diagnose all the reasons for this.

So it was only natural that as a teenager I put together a band, complete with glorious visions of grandeur. We would write hits, win Grammys, blow up bigger than Pearl Jam, and dominate the world.

We never quite achieved world dominance, but we did win second place at the Moncks Corner Fourth of July Festival Battle of the Bands. Take that, Eddie Vedder.

One night after a particularly inspired performance in our backyard, I asked my mom how she liked it. She said it was good, but she said it too much like a mom and not enough like a fan, so I knew she was lying. I pressed her and finally figured out what she didn't like about it when she asked me a simple question: "When are we going to hear *you* sing?"

I was the lead singer, which meant she wasn't talking about her son getting more of the spotlight. She was talking about how, as a singer in a cover band, I was channeling everybody from

Darius Rucker to Billie Joe Armstrong to Van Morrison to Jimi Hendrix. Not horribly, I might add.

She wanted to know, when are we going to hear *you*?

Our lives can be a bit like that. We can spend so much time and energy trying to be like other people that we never let the world hear the real us. What's worse, *we* never hear the real us.

What would happen if we worked half as hard at discovering who we really are as we do at trying to be someone else? How many of us live with buried talents and lost opportunities because we want so badly to be someone we *are not* that we never uncover who we *are*?

Maybe you've heard Jesus's parable about the talents (Matthew 25). By the way, a talent in Hebrew society was a measure of weight, equaling about seventy-five pounds. In this story it symbolizes all our God-given resources—time, money, energy, abilities, and, yes, talents.

In the parable a rich man went away on a long trip and left his estate in the hands of several employees. He gave five talents of gold or silver—imagine five gunnysacks full of bullion or coins—to one person, two talents to another, and one to another.

The employees who received the five talents and the two talents both worked hard, used their resources, and doubled the money. The other guy took a "safer" approach. He dug a hole and buried his talent in the ground.

When the boss returned, he was impressed with the first two men and dismayed by the actions of the last man.

When he asked the third employee why he buried the money, the man's answer was simple: "I was afraid" (verse 25).

Sometimes we do the same thing. We let fear force us into hiding who we are and what we've been given. We bury our identities because we are afraid we don't measure up. We are scared that if we let the real us show, we won't be good enough. We will mess things up. We won't qualify.

So we refuse to use the gifts God has given us. We decline to become the people God made us to be. And to top it off, we congratulate ourselves on being responsible, humble, and wise.

But deep inside, it's simply fear.

This is not a personality thing, by the way. I'm not saying you need to be more of an extrovert or buy a Harley. I'm saying you need to value who you are, and you need to invest yourself in the world around you.

We're all waiting to hear you sing. Sure, you'll mess up sometimes. That's okay. Just like in karaoke, false notes and botched lyrics are some of the best parts.

So I'll ask it again. Who are you? And when are we going to hear the real you?

Just Keeping It Real, Man

Fear isn't the only thing that keeps us from being real. Sometimes we just don't want to admit our weaknesses. You can call it embarrassment, pride, dignity, or ego, but it's never comfortable for our faults to be put on display.

"Keeping it real" is one of those phrases that people use to grant themselves diplomatic immunity in conversation. Maybe you've noticed this. For example, your friend says something that in any other context would have been downright inappropriate or rude, but he chases it with "I'm just keeping it real, bro."

Keeping it real? Is that supposed to soften the blow or cancel the crudeness of what you just said? Because it's not helping, bro.

Keeping it real.

What does that even mean? Sometimes we use authenticity as a cover-up for apathy. I don't think God grants us permission to keep it real by being less than our best. Instead, he wants to familiarize us with the truest version of ourselves. The one who deeply desires to become more and more like him.

The problem with keeping it real is that reality is messy. Chaotic. Flawed. The real you and the real me have a few hiccups.

That's why we prefer the imaginary versions. That's why we fabricate facades and put on personas. Criticism is irritating because it reminds us our flaws are still showing even though we are trying so hard to hide them.

I don't know how to put this politely, so I'm just going to be blunt. Many of us are simply too proud. We call it perfectionism or excellence, but really it's an obsession with never failing. It's an unwillingness to look bad or to admit mistakes. And that makes it hard to be who we really are, because who we are is so far from perfect.

I think it's hilarious that most job applications ask people to list their weaknesses. Everyone knows that you don't write *thief* or *liar* or *chronic whiner* even if it's true. You write things like *workaholic, neat freak,* and *perfectionist.* They should just label that part of the application what it really is:

Humblebrag.

Perfectionism might be a handy faux weakness to list on your job application, but it's not a sustainable lifestyle. And an intolerance of your weaknesses will make it hard to be content with the real you.

At some point we all have to get over our pride and own our deficiencies and dependencies.

I'm not saying to stop working on that temper problem or pessimism in the name of accepting ourselves. Self-confidence isn't an excuse for destructive behavior.

But I am saying that the Christian life is about far more than perfecting ourselves. Perfectionism is the enemy of progress. The impossibility of our perfection is the very reason Jesus died.

The belief that God is more interested in our perfection than our relationship with him is the birthplace of insecurity.

Love You Later

Let me give you a quick pop quiz. Which of these statements is true?

a. God loves us because Jesus died for us.

b. Jesus died for us because God loves us.

The first statement actually sounds pretty spiritual. Jesus redeemed our mess. He died for our unrighteousness. Now God is free to love us. When he sees us, he sees Jesus, and therefore he is pleased. That's why he can love us and put up with us. Right?

Wrong.

If you've read John 3:16, you probably figured out the answer already. God doesn't love us just because Jesus died for us. Jesus died for us because God loved us.

He loved us *first.* Before we did anything and before Jesus did anything. He loved us then and he loves us now because *God is love.* Of all the third words we can ascribe to him, chief among them is *love.*

God's love and mercy came before anything. They motivated him to send Jesus to die for our sins.

The answer, therefore, is *b.* But many of us live as if it were *a,* especially when it comes to dealing with our weaknesses and flaws. We think and talk and act like the only way God can love us is through Jesus.

We think, *Good thing Jesus died for me, because otherwise there's no way God could tolerate me.*

Like most erroneous thinking, there is a kernel of truth in this belief. God is perfectly holy. Clearly we are not. We were sinners who deserved eternal separation from God. Our only hope is the righteousness that Jesus gives us through the Cross. That's the foundation of Christianity.

So from a legal, judicial viewpoint, when God looks at us, he sees Jesus, and that is our saving grace.

But from a relational viewpoint, God doesn't merely tolerate us. He loves us, pursues us, and embraces us.

I think many times we don't believe that, or at least we don't live as if we do. We tend to believe that the only reason God doesn't lose his temper and flick us off the planet is that when he looks at us, he sees us through his Jesus lens. So he takes a deep breath, counts to ten, and withholds the punishment . . . this time.

Meanwhile, we assume God is enamored with the future version of us. The perfect version of us. The impossible version of us. We work as hard as we can to fix ourselves because that's what God really cares about. That's what God expects. That's what we owe him.

But the person we are right now? With our messes, missteps, and mistakes? Not a chance. Our only hope is to hide behind Jesus's grace. It's as if the Cross is some sort of body shield.

And maybe if we can stop smoking, stop cussing, stop yelling at the kids, stop eating ice cream after 9:00 p.m., and actually make something of ourselves, God will be able to embrace us for who we are. He puts up with us for now. He'll love us later.

And maybe when we reach our own goals—that ideal weight, that income level, that standard—we'll be able to love ourselves too.

I can't begin to tell you how flawed and damaging that perspective is.

The Bible teaches the exact opposite. God loved us when we couldn't have cared less about him. How much more certain is his love for us now that we actually want to know him and follow him?

David wrote, "The LORD is like a father to his children, tender and compassionate to those who fear him. For he knows how weak we are; he remembers we are only dust" (Psalm 103:13–14, NLT).

In other words, God isn't intimidated, disgusted, or frustrated with our humanity. He is perfectly comfortable with the messiness that is mankind.

Which begs the question: If we're perfectly accepted as we are, what is our motivation for change?

I love this explanation from theologian Richard Rohr:

> Most of us were taught that God would love us if and when we change. In fact, God loves you so that you can change. What empowers change, what makes you desirous of change, is the experience of love.
>
> It is that inherent experience of love that becomes the engine of change.[4]

The goal of change is not God's love. God's love is the gift that makes the goals possible. When we treat a gift like a goal, both are weakened.

You Heard What?

We just looked at two big reasons we avoid being ourselves: fear of failure and plain old pride. The answer to both is learning to be comfortable with our weaknesses, knowing that God's love and calling don't depend on our perfection.

But there's another reason we don't live up to who we really are, and it's the hardest to spot of them all: *misinformation*.

We have all kinds of third words, and we are thoroughly convinced they are valid. But our self-perception can be based on bad data, and as a result, we never live out what God put inside us.

I have a friend named Wade. One of Wade's claims to fame is that when he was in sixth grade, he was an actor in a series of sex-education videos that were shown in elementary schools all over South Carolina.

That included, of course, Wade's own school, something he hadn't thought about when he signed up for the videos. He is in his late thirties now, and he's never lived it down.

These videos were made circa 1980, so they are very tame. They are also hilariously old-fashioned—to the point that I showed one of them to my church one Sunday morning so we could make fun of my friend together. I have an odd sense of humor, I know.

In this particular video Wade plays the role of a boy named Petey. Petey and his buddy Steve are playing basketball dressed in what I assume to be Bugle Boy jeans and Reebok Pumps. An older man, ostensibly a teacher, is standing to the side, watching. The competition starts to heat up. At one point Steve jumps, and Petey accidentally gets hit in the groin.

Petey gasps. He groans. He stumbles around the court and then collapses on the ground. It was a performance worthy of a South Carolina Oscar.

Steve rushes over and asks in his best *Brady Bunch* voice, "Pete, are you okay? I'm sorry, man."

"Ohhhh. I feel sick."

Immediately the creepy adult rushes over and chimes in. "Hang in there, tiger. I know it hurts. Nothing hurts a guy worse than getting hit in the crotch."

And finally Steve drops the hammer: "Gee, man, you'd better be careful. I've heard getting hit there can cause cancer!"

At which point the teacher/hero addresses Steve with narrowed eyes, asking incredulously, almost menacingly, "You heard *what*?"

And . . . fade to black.

The line "You heard what?" ends up being the point of the video, to encourage kids to get their information from reliable sources.

That's good advice when it comes to sex ed and awkward basketball injuries. And it's not bad advice when it comes to our identities, either.

There are third words rattling around in our heads that we didn't consciously put there. We haven't screened them or approved them. They sneaked in long ago, and there they remain, unchallenged and uncensored.

And sometimes they are dead wrong.

Many of us decided long ago who we were. And it's hard for anyone to tell us otherwise.

Maybe it was something a parent or friend said, and it stuck with us for so long it became part of our psyche. Maybe it was a tragedy or a failure, and the trauma of the moment forever branded us. We promised ourselves we'd never try that again.

When we allow inaccurate third words to program our operating systems, no wonder we feel unqualified. We're evaluating ourselves based on assumptions and accusations that have little or no basis in fact. When we feed our imaginations with distorted memories and unsubstantiated fears, we poison our potential.

It's time to challenge the origin of those third words. It's time to look at yourself a bit incredulously and ask, "You heard *what*?"

First Impressions

I'm sure you've heard the saying "You don't get a second chance to make a first impression."

It's a solid aphorism. If you were heading into an appointment with someone who could end up becoming your spouse or your boss or some other significant figure in the scheme of your existence, you'd want to make the strongest first impression possible. You'd want to iron your sharpest button-down, put your best foot forward, and showcase your strengths. Winning that person's favor could mean a whole new future.

But when it comes to God, the word *impression* doesn't apply. First impressions, second impressions, false impressions, last impressions—they are irrelevant to him because he knows the real you. He sees past the facade and recognizes you for who you really are.

You don't need to impress him to gain his favor. That's a fallacy that haunts Christians and non-Christians alike. Often I find it lurking in the shadows of my own heart. We think we have to clean ourselves up before we draw close to God. We assume his grace and goodness and love belong only to those who have proven themselves worthy.

But that's not the message Jesus brought or the God he modeled.

Look at every human soul Jesus encountered, from the disciples he handpicked, to the sinners he ate dinner with, to the thief he forgave on the cross. Jesus saw the best in people at their worst. He met them in their messes, in their realities, in their most desperate moments. He loved them and believed in them when there was nothing lovable or admirable about them.

You don't need to make a good impression on God.

But you do need to be *honest* with him. And with yourself.

The answer to our identity issues is not found in ourselves. It's found in Jesus. We find our true identities when we filter our third words through the reality of *Christ in us.*

So let's find out what happens when your third words meet God's power.

5

A New Way to Use God's Name

After June 1, 2002, the girl named Holly Boitnott was no more.

Why? Because on that day, which I humbly refer to as "the greatest day of her life," she became Holly Furtick.

What happened when my wife took my name? She didn't just get a new driver's license and passport. She didn't just exchange one impossible-to-pronounce surname for another.

When Holly took my name, she became one with me. Our corporations merged in a sense.

She got the short end of the bargain. That's indisputable.

But anyway, who we are, we are together. What we do, we do together. What we have, we have together.

You took Jesus's name the day you became a Christian. It was, beyond a doubt, the greatest day of *your* life. It was the day you gave him all of you and received all of him in exchange. And it's pretty obvious who got the better side of that deal.

You became one with Jesus. Who he is, you are. What he has, you have.

The apostle John said, "Love has been perfected among us in

this: that we may have boldness in the day of judgment; *because as He is, so are we in this world*" (1 John 4:17, NKJV).

As he is, so are we. In other words, our identity is wrapped up in his. Who we are stems from who he is.

Everything changed the day you took his name.

OMG

Even if that heading made you twitch a little, keep reading.

I'm sure you've heard of the Ten Commandments. You might even have a few of them memorized. They were ten directives that God gave Moses to give to Israel just after they got out of Egypt: *Don't worship other gods. Don't make idols. Don't work on the Sabbath. Obey your parents. Don't kill people. Don't sleep with people you aren't married to. Don't take things that aren't yours. Tell the truth. Don't covet.*

All good stuff, right? All things that most of us would agree on.

But if you're counting, you see I skipped one. It's the one I always misunderstood growing up. It appears in Exodus 20:7: "You shall not *take the name of the LORD your God in vain,* for the LORD will not hold him guiltless who takes His name in vain" (NKJV).

I was always taught this commandment has a very specific and limited application. Basically it boils down to not saying "Oh my God!" when you are shocked or excited. It means not saying "Jesus Christ!" when someone cuts you off in traffic.

As a kid and even as an adult, I couldn't understand why the whole God's-name-in-vain thing was such a big deal. Of all the commandments and principles God could have included, why did this one make the top ten?

If you've been in Christian circles for long, you've probably seen that our applications of this commandment can get a little out of control. For example, a well-meaning gentleman once asked me to go to lunch with him so he could voice a major concern: my inappropriate use of derivative expressions of "the Lord's name in vain." Words like *gosh, golly, gee,* and *jeez.*

I've seen people get combative debating whether OMG is appropriate in text messages.

Gosh, I don't know even how to respond to that. SMH.

In all seriousness, using God's name respectfully in conversation is a good starting place. I agree with that. But this commandment is about far more than how you use God's name as a vocabulary word. It's about how you take his name as *a way of life.* That's how the Hebrews would have understood it.

Do I bear his name appropriately and honorably? Or do I bear it in vain? In other words, do I live according to who he is? Does my life reflect his identity? Or do I live as if I never knew him, never took his name, and never became part of his family?

Unfortunately, my tendency—and maybe yours—is to take this almost as a threat. We think God's focus is our behavior. We feel a bit like a kid who is misbehaving in public, and his parent hisses warnings in his ear while wearing a plastic smile to cover up the fire and brimstone.

"You'd better not embarrass me," we might imagine God saying. "You'd better act like me and talk like me and represent me properly."

But our actions are only a small part of what it means to take God's name in vain and are the least important in the long run.

In reality, this commandment is directly connected to our third words. To our identities. To how we view ourselves.

Remember, God's name is I AM. So anytime we take his name and fill in the third word with things that are contradictory to what God says about us, we are taking his name in vain. When we allow our third words to override his third words, we are treating his name as empty and hollow.

Maybe you think or say, "I am . . . pathetic."

But God responds with *You might feel that way, but you took my name. And I am . . . powerful. And if I am in you, you aren't pathetic anymore. You have all the power that's in my name.*

Do you see how revolutionary this is? It is not a threat to bludgeon us into obedience. It is permission to act like who we really are . . . *in him*.

God is giving us the gift of identity.

His identity.

His sufficiency.

His qualifications.

God wants to give you his name in your situation, in your weakness, and in your need.

But you have to take it.

You have to learn to use it.

How to Be Your Selfie

Our identity starts with, and depends on, God's identity.

A. W. Tozer wrote, "What comes into our minds when we think about God is the most important thing about us."[5]

God defines us. Who he is fills in the blanks of who we are. Our concept of God trickles down into every facet of life, carving and coloring our identity. It determines the third words we believe about ourselves and the third words we reject.

Not only is it impossible to separate who we are from who God is, but it's also dangerous. J. I. Packer warned in his book *Knowing God*:

> The world becomes a strange, mad, painful place, and life in it a disappointing and unpleasant business, for those who do not know about God. Disregard the study of God, and you sentence yourself to stumble and blunder through life blindfolded, as it were, with no sense of direction, and no understanding of what surrounds you. This way you can waste your life and lose your soul.[6]

The idea that we can find ourselves without first finding God is a fallacy. It is ignorance and arrogance masquerading as self-enlightenment. "Discovering yourself" is an immensely popular pastime in our culture. But on its own it's an endeavor that is doomed to fail.

The very terms we use highlight the problem: self-help,

self-esteem, self-discovery, self-fulfillment, self-improvement, self-acceptance.

What's the commonality?

Self.

Yet self is the wrong starting point.

I wouldn't say self is the problem, either. I'm not advocating that we abandon our individuality and become clones of some illusive, intangible concept of the perfect person.

But if we really want to discover ourselves, if we really want to find out whether we are qualified, we have to look beyond ourselves. We have to look to the One who created us.

Sure, even without God we can understand ourselves, in part. We can explore our temperaments and personalities. We can define our likes and dislikes. We can list our aptitudes and ineptitudes. We can feel our way through our emotional labyrinths and delve deep into our buried traumas.

There is a place for all that. I'm not against counselors or psychiatrists or self-help. They exist precisely because this whole question of identity is so deeply ingrained in us.

But apart from God, it's impossible to get a clear picture of who we are, because our identity is so intimately and intricately and inseparably bound to his.

That's not a particularly popular concept in a culture defined by self. A culture absorbed with image and polish and poise. A culture obsessed with casting off restraint and controlling one's own destiny.

But in reality it is incredibly freeing.

When you discover who God is, you discover who you are. And when you discover who you are, you no longer have to struggle with the insecurity and self-promotion that define much of society. You no longer have to strain to measure up, to qualify.

You are free to be yourself.

The apostle Paul described the situation this way: "For now we see through a glass, darkly; but then face to face: now I know in part; but then shall I know even as also I am known" (1 Corinthians 13:12, KJV).

That's the third word that unlocks all the others.

I am . . . *known.* By whom? A patient, kind, omniscient God.

Looking at yourself through any other window guarantees a distorted picture.

Life's Biggest Question

So if discovering God's identity is so important, how do we find out who God is? How can we comprehend the invisible, eternal, all-powerful, all-knowing Creator of the universe? How do we relate to the God who bends time and space and gravity to his will? Especially when there are infinite interpretations that often violently contradict one another?

It sounds intimidating.

But it doesn't have to be.

When it comes to finding God, we don't have to look very hard. He revealed himself to us in Jesus. For thirty-three years Jesus walked this planet, showing us how God thinks, talks, and loves.

Interestingly, Jesus revealed himself to Israel using exactly the same name God used with Moses thousands of years earlier: I AM.

The story is found in John 8. In the context Jesus was having a heated discussion with a group of Israelites about who he was and why he came. They were confused, and nothing Jesus said seemed to get through to them.

But the last straw came when Jesus hinted that he knew Abraham, who of course had been dead for a couple of millenniums.

His listeners mockingly asked him how he could have seen Abraham when he wasn't even fifty years old yet.

Jesus replied, "Very truly I tell you, . . . before Abraham was born, I am!" (verse 58).

I am. There are those two words again. The words that define and redefine our existence. The words that set up our third words and invite us to live in God's identity.

Jesus wasn't trying to be confusing. He was trying to tell them that he was God.

It was that simple.

Jesus is the I AM. God is the I AM. Therefore Jesus is God.

Jesus wanted his listeners to understand that he was the person they had been waiting for. He was the answer to their needs, their fears, their weaknesses, their sins.

He was the way *to* God, because he *was* and *is* God.

Later in his ministry Jesus had a conversation about his identity with Simon Peter, and Jesus asked him an all-important question. Here is how Matthew described the conversation:

> When Jesus came to the region of Caesarea Philippi, he asked his disciples, "Who do people say the Son of Man is?"
>
> They replied, "Some say John the Baptist; others say Elijah; and still others, Jeremiah or one of the prophets."
>
> "But what about you?" he asked. "Who do you say I am?"
>
> Simon Peter answered, "You are the Messiah, the Son of the living God."
>
> Jesus replied, "Blessed are you, Simon son of Jonah, for this was not revealed to you by flesh and blood, but by my Father in heaven. And I tell you that you are Peter, and on this rock I will build my church, and the gates of Hades will not overcome it." (16:13–18)

Simon knew the right answer to Jesus's question. Jesus was the Messiah, the Savior, God.

That was a big moment for Simon, actually, because he had a history of putting his foot in his mouth. But this time, when it really mattered, he got it right.

Who do you say that Jesus is?

It's life's biggest question. Getting this question right is both the quintessence of salvation and the starting point for a lifelong journey.

We are saved when we come to know and believe in Jesus as our Lord and Savior, but that is only the beginning of our relationship with him. Knowing God as he is really is paramount to finding out why he made us and who he means for us to be.

That question leads us to a second question:

Who do you say that you are?

What we think about Jesus is foundational to what we think about ourselves. When Simon correctly identified who Jesus was, Jesus identified who Simon was. "I tell you that *you are Peter,* and on *this rock* I will build my church" (verse 18).

Until that point the fisherman from the village of Bethsaida had always gone by Simon. From then on, though, he was known as Rock. That's what *petros,* or Peter, means in Greek. Not a bad nickname. It suggested that Peter, even with his all-too-obvious imperfections, would be foundational to the movement Jesus was establishing.

Upon Simon's confession of Jesus's identity, Jesus gave him a new confession to make about his own identity.

Before . . .

I was Simon.

Now . . .

I am Rock.

What changed in that moment wasn't who Peter was but rather his *view* of who he was.

Jesus said he was a rock. This meant he was qualified.

Suddenly Peter had hope. He had a future. He could see the man he really was and the man he was becoming because Jesus changed his third word.

"You are Peter."

God wants to give us a revelation of who we are. He wants to show us our value now, and he wants to open our eyes to who we can become in him.

But here's what's sobering. A lot of us come to the point of making a correct theological assertion about who Jesus is without ever making the connection between who he is and who we are now in him.

We know the right theology, but we haven't applied it to our lives and lifestyles. We are essentially taking his name in vain. Not because we don't value him or honor him, but because we don't realize how powerfully his name can permeate our present and transform our existence.

We might be saved and headed to heaven, but until we get our third words right, we'll wander disoriented and distracted through our lives on this planet. We'll waste time and resources and energy and dreams.

I believe God wants to take us on an adventure of God-discovery and self-discovery. It is a journey that will lead to fulfillment as we have never imagined.

Along the way I think one thing will stand out: most of the time our third words aren't big enough. They don't do God justice. We settle for mediocrity because it's believable and achievable and because it's what we think we deserve. But God has so much more in store for us. It comes with the name. It's part of the deal.

Do you believe Jesus died for *you*? That his sacrifice paid for your guilt and shame once and for all? That it brought you into God's family as a son or daughter with full rights and privileges? Do you believe that God could never love you more or less than he does right now, no matter what you do or don't do?

If so, then it's time to live like it.

Often we don't take Jesus into account when we fill in our

third words. So the words and phrases we use to describe ourselves end up being too small, too limited, too conditional, and too apologetic.

God wants to blow the lid off your expectations of yourself. Stop talking about who you are not and what you cannot do, and start listening to what God says about your life. Stop labeling yourself, and start letting God do whatever he wants in and through and with you.

WDJSAM

Understanding who Jesus is isn't just an ethereal question to ponder late at night when you're trying to sleep. It isn't just a topic for pundits to debate and professors to pontificate about.

It hits at the heart of who you are and how you live, especially when you are dealing with the fallout from your own humanity.

Maybe you just screwed up at work again, and now you find yourself fired again. It's become a pattern, and you hate yourself for it.

Maybe you've lived beyond your income, playing accounts and creditors like Vegas, but now your debt has found you, and bankruptcy is a specter on your doorstep.

Maybe you cheated on your spouse, and now you can't regain the trust you betrayed. You let down the person who depended on you the most, and you don't know if you can ever fix the mess you made.

Maybe you had an opportunity to advance your career but you listened to fear and didn't take the risk. You missed the moment, and now you're frustrated because it seems as if you're always too slow, too timid, too insecure.

And you wonder, *Am I really pleasing to God? Can he accept who I am even when the real me is broken and flawed and disqualified and so . . . stinking . . . human?*

If it's hard for you to believe that God could love and accept you, try thinking about Jesus's opinion of you. After all, Jesus came to reveal God's heart. So what Jesus thinks about you is what God thinks about you.

Remember the WWJD bracelets? Michelle Haynes bought me one when I was sixteen, and I wore it until both Ws wore off. A multimillion-dollar industry was spawned out of one simple question: *What would Jesus do?*

And, of course, there are all kinds of spin-offs. What would Jesus drive? What would Jesus eat? And a personal favorite, What would Scooby do?

WWJD. It's a great question, and in a moment of indecision, confusion, or temptation, it can help you figure out which path to take.

I agree that what we *do* is important. But who we *are* is even more important. What we do always follows who we are—or who we think we are. So there is a better question to ask: *What does Jesus say about me?*

The acronym WDJSAM might not be quite as catchy. But the answer to that question will revolutionize your existence, just as it did Peter's.

What does Jesus say about you? About your problems? About your needs? About your sins?

If you read the Gospels, it doesn't take long to realize that Jesus was really good at loving and helping problematic people. Look at his life. Look at the people he talked to and ate with and hung out with. Look at how he reacted to people in sin. That is how he reacts to you, and that is what he thinks about you.

Jesus came to put hands and feet on God's love for broken mankind. Jesus loved to be with mean people, selfish people, addicted people, and bad people. He wasn't turned off by the stigma or the stench. He spent his days with the rejected and the ruined. He met people in their messes, and his wholehearted acceptance and love changed them forever.

Remember the woman caught in adultery? You may know the story. It's found in John 8, and it is one of the most revealing moments of Jesus's ministry.

Somehow a few religious leaders caught this woman in the act of sin, in the very definition of immorality. They decided they would make an example of her. They would expose her failures publicly in order to trap Jesus.

So the religious leaders dragged her before Jesus and asked him what should be done. Should they stone her as the Law required? Or let her go and flout justice?

If you've read the story, you know what happened next. Jesus didn't condemn her. If anything, he condemned her condemners. He pointed out that, in reality, they weren't any holier than the woman. They needed grace and mercy and hope just as much as she did.

So one by one they slunk away in silent shame. Here's the end of the story:

> Jesus straightened up and asked her, "Woman, where are they? Has no one condemned you?"
>
> "No one, sir," she said.
>
> "Then neither do I condemn you," Jesus declared. "Go now and leave your life of sin." (verses 10–11)

I can't overstate the significance of Jesus's treatment of this woman and her sin. It was the polar opposite of how the Jews expected God to react.

To them, God was a God of holiness, of righteousness, and of judgment. He was a perfect God who cared about the tiniest details of the Law. That was the message the Pharisees hammered into the people.

Again, this understanding is built on elements of truth: God is a holy God, and sin is an affront to his nature. Sin separates mankind from God, and it deserves punishment and death.

That is precisely why Jesus came to the planet. He wasn't here to judge this woman. He was here to save her. He wasn't her prosecutor. He was her defense lawyer.

So he let her go.

Was justice mocked? No, because ultimately he knew he would bear the punishment for the sin she was guilty of committing as well as every sin committed by every human throughout history. Including mine. Including yours.

How does Jesus react to our sin? The same way he reacted in this instance. He defends us. He protects us. He dispels our accusers. And he gives us hope that we can live differently in the future.

What is fascinating to me about this woman is we don't even know her name. We always call her "the woman caught in adultery."

Talk about a label. She is forever defined by her biggest blunder.

At least to us.

But that's not how Jesus saw her that day. It's not what God named her.

I think when we get to heaven, we'll ask to meet this person named The Woman Caught in Adultery.

And people will say, "Who? There's no one here by that name. Oh wait . . . Do you mean the person named The Woman Who Wasn't Judged for Her Adultery? The one who's known around here as The Woman Jesus Forgave? The person we like to call The Woman Who Went and Sinned No More? She's right over there. She goes by a different name now."

While we're at it, I have a friend who once visited a church where they call this Bible passage "The Story of the Men Caught Throwing Stones." Nice.

Don't get me wrong: I'm not saying mistakes don't matter. Sin is terrible. Loss and failure and tragedy hurt like crazy. So I'm not glossing over pain or excusing sin.

But look at how Jesus loved people, and apply that to your circumstances and your reality. Let God's love, which is personified in Jesus, fill in your third words. Learn to look at yourself through his eyes. Filter your self-definitions and self-evaluations through the lenses of God's mercy, goodness, and power. Let him decide what qualifies you.

John summed up Jesus's mission like this: "God did not send his Son into the world to condemn the world, but to save the world through him" (John 3:17).

That is still his mission. Two thousand years later he is still wholeheartedly committed to saving the world, not condemning the world, through Jesus.

When you come face to face with your failure, it's far too easy to give up on yourself. To accept the labels and limits and lids that your past might seem to require.

I am sinful.

I am unfaithful.

I am addicted.

I am disgraceful.

I am unworthy.

But in Christ your accusers are gone. And the one whose opinion matters most stands before you, a smile on his face and tenderness in his eyes. He tells you there is hope. There is a future. You can live a different kind of life. You can become the person he meant for you to be.

EMBRACE TO REPLACE

I have weaknesses, and you do too. We've established that. But that can't be the end of the story. What do we do about them?

Do we live with them?

Do we deny them?

Do we pray about them?

Do we fix them?

Not so long ago I thought I knew the answer to those questions. Actually, I had *two* answers.

The problem was, they were contradictory.

6

The Opposite of God

My boys, Elijah and Graham, being siblings, males, and offspring of their father, are slightly competitive. And by *slightly* I mean extremely, violently, throw-each-other-across-the-room-if-need-be competitive.

They are currently ages ten and eight. Every morning when I wake up and walk out of my bedroom, they race to give me a hug. I can hear them coming before I see them.

That sounds sweet, but it's not. This has nothing to do with childlike love or boundless enthusiasm to greet dear old Dad.

It's a race. It's a hunt.

And I am simultaneously the finish line and the prey.

These are the most brutal hugs imaginable. I've learned to brace myself. I've considered keeping a protective cup bedside.

Competition and comparison seem to come with the territory. Neither brother would ever concede that the other has some qualities or strengths or advantages. That would be admitting defeat.

So no matter what compliment I give either of them, the other one figures out how to diffuse it.

Sometimes just to provoke a little banter (what is wrong with me?), I'll pose a question like this: "Elijah, don't you think Graham is the strongest eight-year-old in the world?"

And he'll reply, "Yeah, if it's opposite day."

Opposite day. A clever way to turn everything I just said on its head and become the champion of that particular verbal joust.

Actually, though, God is the founder of opposite day. Not in the sense of negativity or contradiction, of course. God isn't out to frustrate or provoke us. But God has a sneaky way of doing the opposite of what we expect or deserve. His values and priorities are different from ours. His thoughts are higher than ours.

And without fail what God does even through our weaknesses is bigger and better and bolder than we could have asked or thought.

When we look at our shortcomings and mistakes, we tend to resign ourselves to where we are. *I'll never succeed,* we think. *My best efforts are too little, too late. There is no hope.*

But God smiles. And he replies, "Normally, that would be true—in your own strength. But I'm officially declaring this to be opposite day. So everything negative you've spoken about yourself has been turned on its head. You thought you were weak, but actually you are strong. You thought you had failed, but I'm preparing you for your greatest success. You thought you were disqualified, but your calling is surer than ever. It's opposite day."

It's a silly illustration, and I understand it could come across a bit simplistic. But understanding God's ability and propensity to do the opposite of what we deserve has transformed me. It's liberated me. It's revolutionized how I process weaknesses and failures, both my own and those of others.

It's the heart of what I am saying in this book.

Too often we take stock of our negative third words and give up in despair. Our problems are painfully apparent and our failures agonizingly obvious. So we file our dreams under "fairy tale." We are who we are, and we fear nothing can change that.

Yet deep in our souls we know there has to be hope. We read the Bible and see a God of miracles, of resurrection power, of impossible odds. Something inside tells us to try again and believe again.

So what do we do with our weaknesses? How do we react to the facts that we are flawed and our flaws seem to be disqualifying us from our dreams?

As I mentioned earlier, there are two possible answers to that question, but they're difficult to reconcile.

One answer is to *embrace* who we are. The Bible has a lot to say about that: about our humility, about our lost condition, about our need for God, and about finding our value in Jesus. You can make a solid biblical case for admitting and embracing even your least flattering third words.

The problem with that is it seems to sell short God's power to transform us. It sentences us to the prison of our present condition.

Are we really supposed to resign ourselves to who we are, with our damaging and destructive tendencies? Do we simply determine to love ourselves more? Do we redefine good and bad so we can feel better about the current us, the real us, the version of us that we have to deal with every day?

That doesn't seem right. That's not the God we see in the Bible. We aren't helpless, hopeless, pitiful victims. We are more than conquerors in Jesus.

The second answer is to *replace* our weaknesses with strengths. It's to let God transform us, fix us, and change us. To erase our third words and let God's words fill in our blanks. To double down in our commitment to relentlessly exchange bad for good. To struggle against our flaws and fight to fix ourselves.

That solution has its own problems, though. In our effort to get rid of all our weaknesses and replace them with strengths, we can end up reducing the Christian walk to a self-help program. And in the process we set ourselves up for a lifetime of disappointment, because we will never fix everything. Meanwhile, we open ourselves up to the kind of self-loathing and impatience that is completely counterproductive to change.

These two options—embrace or replace—sound mutually exclusive. It's either one or the other. When we come face to face with our weaknesses, are we supposed to accept them or reject them? Give up on them or get busy fixing them?

As a pastor I've often found myself giving conflicting advice. Sometimes my counsel has been the "Don't be so hard on yourself; let go and let God" variety. Other times I'm explaining that "It's up to you to change; the key is your initiative."

Actually, this book grew out of that inherent tension in dealing with weaknesses. I started to wonder why in the world changing humans—including myself—is so complicated. And the more I studied the Bible, the more I realized this isn't a new problem. The greatest heroes of the faith struggled with the most basic weaknesses and temptations.

I began to realize that my pat answers didn't do justice to the complexity of the human condition.

Worse than that, they didn't do justice to God.

The answer to the embrace/replace dichotomy is not as nice and neat and comfortable as I once thought. But it's all throughout the Bible, and it's as powerful as it is practical. Once you see it, it will do far more than just change your behavior or build your self-esteem.

It will set you free to be the real you, the you that God created you to be.

It's a glorious, organic, lifelong process. And it relentlessly points us to God instead of to self. To grace instead of straining. To faith rather than rules.

When I Am Weak

Recently I was in my office reading a passage in 2 Corinthians 12 when the proverbial light bulb came on.

In the passage Paul was talking about some of his personal struggles. He expressed in no uncertain terms how frustrated he was with his weakness. He actually called it a thorn in his flesh and a messenger from Satan.

We don't know what the problem was. It could have been eye

trouble or persecution or depression or his mother-in-law or any number of things. Okay, he wasn't married, so the mother-in-law theory doesn't work.

The point is that the weakness was *real*. And it was affecting Paul and his ministry. It was limiting his influence and effectiveness. By our standards it was a problem that needed to be eliminated. That was the only logical conclusion.

So here was the greatest author in the New Testament, the apostle who was forcibly removed from his donkey by Jesus and shown heavenly visions, the guy who opened the door of the gospel to the entire Gentile world, and he was confused and confined by a weakness.

We can assume that by this point Paul had already done everything in his power to change the situation. There's nothing wrong with trying to solve our problems, by the way. God gave us brains for a reason.

But in this case it wasn't enough. So Paul did what any of us would do. He asked God to fix it. Three times.

It's safe to say that by the third time this wasn't just a polite request. Paul probably begged and pleaded and cajoled and maybe even tried to manipulate a little.

We've all done that, I'm sure. Foxhole prayers are a long and revered tradition among Christians and non-Christians alike.

But it didn't work. Nothing changed. Nothing improved.

Each time he went to God in prayer, God spoke this to him: "My grace is sufficient for you, for my power is made perfect in weakness" (verse 9).

That wasn't exactly what Paul wanted to hear.

That's why he kept praying.

It was a profoundly unsatisfying response because Paul was human. He had the same worries as we do. The same needs for security and control and affirmation that we have.

What we *want* to hear from God is this: "Thanks for alerting me to your malfunction! I'll get on that right away." And then we want him to wave his hand and eliminate our shortcomings by the end of the business day, please.

Instead, he gives us this mysterious promise that his power works best when we are weak. We don't really know what that means most of the time, so it's less than comforting. It certainly doesn't offer much in the way of practical application.

But as I read this passage that day, I could identify with Paul. I could sense his frustration, because it's mine as well. Why do I have to have weaknesses? Wouldn't I be much more effective for God if I were perfect?

Then I saw something that stopped me in my tracks.

He wrote in verse 10, "For when I am weak, then I am strong."

Something clicked in my head. I read that phrase again and again and again. I realized something. Here in front of me were Paul's own *I am* statements. His own third words.

Do you see them?

When . . .

I am weak

Then . . .

I am strong.

Weak and *strong* are both Paul's third words.

Are we supposed to be weak? Or are we supposed to be strong? Paul figured out the answer.

It's both *at the same time.*

Notice, Paul didn't say, "I used to be weak, but now I'm strong." Or "If I could ever stop being weak, then finally I'd be strong." It isn't about being strong *despite* weaknesses. It isn't about being strong *after* weaknesses are gone.

It is about being strong *in* and *through* and *because* of weaknesses.

God doesn't want us to embrace our weakness to the point of resigning ourselves to a life of failure and defeat. Nor does he want us to stress and fret over replacing every weakness with strength before we step into our destiny.

We can be weak and strong at the same time. And I'll go even further than that. Our weaknesses can actually become our strengths.

Who we are right now—with our weaknesses and strengths, our failures and successes—is not the problem. Who we are is the solution. Somehow, incredibly, those things that drive us crazy about ourselves might be central to the fulfillment of our potential.

Our weaknesses don't disqualify us. They actually qualify us even more, because they are the portals through which God's power permeates our lives.

That doesn't mean you never need to change, of course. Actually, you never stop changing.

But it means the current version of you is the right version of you for this moment. It means you can stop stressing and straining to be a different you, because the real you is perfect and priceless. It's not only what God has to work with. It's what God wants to work with.

And from that starting place, progress is possible.

Recently I was reading Gretchen Rubin's book titled *Better Than Before.* It's about how our hard-wired tendencies toward expectations affect our habits. When considering which tendencies are the most preferable in human beings, she offers this insight: "The happiest and most successful people are those who have figured out ways to exploit their Tendency to their benefit and, just as important, found ways to counterbalance its limitations."[7]

I like the thought that it's not the tendencies I'm born with that determine my ability to grow. It's my relationship with those tendencies.

I'll say it again: it's not about embracing versus replacing. It's not one or the other. Somehow it's both.

We embrace who we are to become who we were meant to be. We embrace to replace.

When I am weak, then I am strong.

The more I read that phrase, the more excited I became. It was like a master key that unlocked many of the things I had been learning about God.

My mind started racing to several Bible characters I had been studying lately.

People like Moses, who stuttered so badly he was convinced God could never use him but who ended up becoming one of the greatest leaders in human history.

People like Rahab and Ruth and Jeremiah and Paul himself, who all seemed so disqualified, yet they found strength in their weaknesses.

And then, of course, there is the antihero Jacob. The guy was a liar and a cheat but somehow ended up being a key player in God's redemptive plan for humanity.

The writer of Hebrews understood that principle. In Hebrews 11 he listed a who's who of Bible heroes. In some ways they are so embarrassingly fallible that you have to wonder who was running the Hall of Faith induction committee. He capped off the chapter with this:

> And what more shall I say? I do not have time to tell about Gideon, Barak, Samson and Jephthah, about David and Samuel and the prophets, who through faith conquered kingdoms, administered justice, and gained what was promised; who shut the mouths of lions, quenched the fury of the flames, and escaped the edge of the sword; *whose weakness was turned to strength.* (verses 32–34)

There it is again. *Weakness . . . turned to strength.*

Apparently Paul's case wasn't a fluke. This is God's modus operandi, his standard operating procedure. His signature riff, if you will.

God doesn't just ignore or bypass our weaknesses, and he certainly doesn't let himself be stopped by them. He faces them head-on and turns them into strengths.

That's how big and good and sovereign God is.

Uniquely Weak

Wait, you might be thinking, *are you suggesting that I don't have to fix anything? That God is okay with my sins? I don't have to do anything because somehow God will magically turn sins into strengths?*

Not at all. The Bible is full of exhortations to change, to stop sinning, to overcome temptation, and to challenge strongholds.

What I'm saying is that our response to weaknesses is not always as cut-and-dried as simply embracing or replacing. It's more complicated than that, just as our identities themselves are complicated. When we face specific weaknesses, we have to figure out what God wants us to do with them.

First, some things need to be embraced. Accepted. Tolerated. They aren't going away, so we might as well get used to the idea. We need to learn to compensate for them, we need to lean on others, and mostly we need to have a healthy dose of humility.

Second, some things need to be replaced immediately. They are *not* part of our God-given identities. They are interlopers and intruders. They are hurting us or others, and God wants to help us eradicate them now.

Third, other things need to be replaced . . . eventually. We can start now, but the process could take years. We need to develop patience and, again, humility.

In some cases it's easy to tell which of these categories a certain fault or failure fits into, especially when the weakness is obviously a sin. For example, we don't need to pray about whether murder, adultery, or lying should be part of our lives for the next thirty years. The Bible calls them sin, and God gives us power to live differently now that we know him.

But most of our weaknesses are a little fuzzier. Often they are a matter of degrees or context.

For example, let's say you are an introvert. Does that need to change? Is that a weakness?

Well, it's hard to say. God doesn't want you to live in fear, and sometimes shyness is a result of paralyzing fear. So to the extent fear rules your life, that's probably a weakness that God would like to help you overcome.

And if the fear limits you so much that you don't obey God's will for your life, or if you are somehow hurting others with your silence, then you could argue that it's a sin and that God wants to set you free.

But even if you conquered fear and became the most confident, brave, secure person around, would you ever be an extrovert? Probably not. That's not who you were made to be.

Being introverted is a beautiful personality trait, and as such, it is a *strength,* not a weakness. Spending your life trying to be an extrovert when God created you to be an introvert is just as big a travesty as being a fear-bound recluse.

So, dear theoretical introvert, you get to choose how to respond. You get to sort out—with God's help—whether you need to change dramatically, moderately, or not at all.

Let me give you another example. Maybe you wish you were more spontaneous. You admire the way more fun-loving people are able to make memories with those they love because they're willing to go off script. In fact, you envy their openness. But should you emulate it if your personality inclines you to plan . . . everything?

Maybe you could experiment with some different approaches. Get a little wild and crazy and decide what really needs planning, what is overkill, and what is an unhealthy need for control. But this doesn't mean holding yourself hostage to an expectation of spontaneity beyond your makeup. That will only drain you of the strength you need to enjoy the things you plan so brilliantly.

Do you see how individualized this process is? Your weaknesses are as unique as your strengths. And as such, they deserve some respect.

Oswald Chambers said, "Unguarded strength is actually a double weakness."[8]

But do we realize that a misunderstood weakness might also be a forfeited strength?

It's worth taking the time to evaluate your third words humbly and honestly in light of God's power at work in you. Don't be too quick to excuse your sin, but don't be too quick to label your quirks as faults and try to change them, either.

The key is knowing who you are to God. As you discover his definition of the real you, you will know how to respond to your unique needs and problems.

So how do you evaluate your weaknesses? How do you know if you are meant to grow in a particular area? Here are a few questions to help you decide.

Does the Bible call my weakness sin?

If so, God wants to help you work through that. Sin is not part of who you really are. It's an alien and a parasite. Since it's not part of who you were meant to be, you can change with God's help. Again, that could take a while, so don't give up too soon. Keep resisting temptation and responding to God's grace throughout the process.

Having said that, let me emphasize that the presence of sin doesn't automatically disqualify you from pursuing God's plan for your life. If that were the case, we'd all be hopelessly disqualified, because we all sin. God blesses us despite our sins, and he is sovereign enough and good enough to use even our mistakes for his glory.

On the other hand, if your weakness isn't clearly a sin, maybe you don't need to be in such a hurry to eradicate it. Your first step is to figure out whether God wants you change it or to simply embrace who you are and allow him to be strong in your weakness.

Do I want to overcome this weakness or grow in this area?

God says that he gives us both "the desire and the power" to do his will (Philippians 2:13, NLT). If you have a deep-seated desire to do something, be someone, or change in some way, chances are high that God put the desire there, and he will help you achieve it—even against crazy odds. Your desires aren't infallible, of course, but if you are following God, often you will instinctively know what is best for your life. You might just need to trust yourself (and God in you) a little more.

Do I have grace to change?

Grace is God's supernatural power in your life. Usually you can tell fairly quickly if you have grace to grow or to change in a particular area, because things click. You invest time and energy into something, and God breathes on it. It feels natural and fulfilling. The Christian life is not meant to be next to impossible, by the way. Jesus said his yoke is easy and his burden is light (see Matthew 11:30).

What do other people say about my weaknesses and strengths?

What people notice about you can be incredibly revealing. The key is to know whom to listen to. You need people in your life who understand you, sharpen you, challenge you, and encourage you. When you find people like that, listen to what they say they see in you. You might be surprised how little your weaknesses bother other people and how obvious your strengths are to them. Sometimes our third words need to be calibrated by asking those around us for their evaluation.

The Author's Antonyms

We usually assume that if God wants to replace our third words, he'll do so with terms that are clear opposites.

I am exhausted might become *I am energized.*

I am hurt might become *I am healed.*

I am trapped might become *I am free.*

Sometimes that's true. But if you look at Scripture, you'll see that God's opposites are often different from ours.

God is subtler. Sneakier. And far more effective.

When we follow God, he makes us a new creation on a spiritual level, but that doesn't mean he obliterates our personalities or bulldozes our natural identities. He doesn't knock everything over and start rebuilding from the ground up. He seems to prefer to work with what he has in front of him. After all, the original material came from him, so it must be good stuff.

By overlaying his own third words over ours, he brings our real identities to light.

Do you remember those secret decoders they used to hide in cereal boxes? They were little frames or cardboard glasses with a red film. The idea was to use the decoder to look at particular images, which at first appeared to be nonsensical. When you did, the red film would filter out the background, and secret messages would appear.

As a kid I begged my mom to buy those cereals, not because I particularly liked them and certainly not because of their nutritional content, but because I wanted those decoders. I wanted to know what message was hiding on the back of that box.

That's a little bit like what happens when God lays his third words over ours. Suddenly the nonsense makes sense. The illogical finds meaning. We see ourselves differently because we are looking through God's eyes. And the messages we receive are a good deal more profound than what you get from Kix.

Sometimes we beg God to eliminate our shortcomings and replace them with the opposite. But God would rather give us his third words. And when we look at life through that filter, everything changes.

Let me give you some examples.

Maybe the most glaring third word you hear in your mind right now is this: *I am failing.* Of course, you might use other, more colorful descriptors: *I am a loser. I am a disaster. I am a catastrophe. I suck at life.* But it all comes back to failure.

So you assume that God wants to make you a success. After all, success is the opposite of failure, so if failure is the problem, success is the answer.

But God might have a different plan.

When we feel like failures, God's third word for us is often this: *I am growing.* That is not as ego boosting as *I am successful.* But it's a lot more real. And when you think about it, it's even more powerful.

Success is temporary and superficial. And somewhat arbitrary. No one is successful at everything all the time. So if your identity rests on the outcome of your efforts, you are setting yourself up for a lot of self-doubt and pain.

You aren't failing; you are growing. And you aren't a failure; you are a person who is continually improving. Yes, your failures are real, but they aren't final. They can actually work for you in the future. Rather than defining yourself by them, define yourself by what God is accomplishing through them. That is a far healthier approach to life.

Here's another one: *I am unworthy.* That was the third word my brother Max struggled with.

The logical opposite of that is *I am worthy.* But in our culture, *worthy* is usually equated with *deserving.* As we've already seen, none of us could deserve God's love, forgiveness, and blessings.

So what is God's opposite of *unworthy*? We could probably list several, but here's one of my favorites: *I am accepted.*

If you think you have to swap *unworthy* for *worthy,* you will bang your forehead against a self-created wall for the rest of your life, and you'll never get any closer to your goal. But once you realize that God's acceptance overrules your unworthiness, you can instantly find peace.

Your sins and shortcomings don't separate you from God, because he has accepted you through your faith in Jesus. You are preapproved through Jesus, not through your own works or performance.

Maybe you keep making mistakes, the same mistakes. And it's progressively harder to come back to God, because each time you do, you realize how many times you've promised to change . . . but failed. Your optimism and your motivation are at an all-time low.

Stop focusing on your unworthiness, and focus instead on God's acceptance. Thank him for reaching out to you in your place of need and for loving you unconditionally. Recognize and rehearse his unmerited favor in your life.

Then get back up and try again.

The Enemy's biggest win isn't when he gets you to sin. He wins biggest when he gets you to lose sight of God's acceptance of you. When he convinces you that your righteousness and relationship with God hang on your actions, you stay in a spiral of shame.

Instead of trying to contradict your unworthiness, embrace it. But then replace it with God's acceptance and approval.

Or maybe your third word is *I am afraid.* What is the opposite of fear? Is it courage? Bravery?

Those things are good, but here's one you might not have thought of: *love.*

Try saying *I am loving* instead of saying *I am afraid.* Focus changes everything. The more you focus on others, the more your fear will fade into the background. Fearful is what you feel, but loving is who God has made you to be.

We just listed three negative third words and some possible ways to replace them, but they are only the beginning. We all have personal struggles, and God has the perfect opposite for each one of them.

It's not my goal or my role to tell you all the third words God has for you. That's your own, very personal journey with God. But I will say this: keep your eyes open for God's unexpected opposites.

Life is a journey of discovery and change. Of learning to listen to God's third words more than your own. Of discovering how to face your flaws with honesty and faith.

You may not feel qualified for the journey. At one point or another, we all feel ridiculously unqualified for what God has called us to do. That's okay. Actually, it's preferable and maybe even essential. God loves to work with unqualified people.

You can't experience God's strength, though, until you learn to let down your guard. Your humility opens the door for your weaknesses to become strengths, as we will see in the next chapter.

Heaven's Secret Weapon

When it comes to our weaknesses, we tend to oscillate between two extremes, both of which stem from insecurity. We wallow in our weaknesses, or we try to pretend they don't exist.

We talked about the first extreme when we discussed our identities and our third words, and we'll look at it more in the following pages. The problem with the "Woe is me" approach to weakness is that we authorize ourselves to contradict God's calling on our lives. Effectively, we deputize ourselves as the qualifier. And as we've seen, our self-assessment can be wildly inaccurate.

But many times we err on the other side: pretending our weaknesses don't exist. We try to hide our flaws from God, others, and even ourselves. The problem with this is that until we admit our needs, God can't do much to help us. Greatness is birthed from humility, not denial. Weaknesses become strengths when they are embraced, not ignored.

Sometimes we assume—or maybe we've been taught—that a person who really loves God never settles for less than perfection. We have to have positive thoughts, positive confessions, and positive actions.

I'm all in favor of positivity. But I'm dead set against dishonesty, even when it's ourselves we're lying to.

Admitting our weaknesses is not doubt, fear, or lack of faith. Actually, it is one of the clearest signs that we have faith. It means that our confidence is placed in God, not ourselves. It means we are secure enough in who *he is* to admit who *we are not.*

On the other hand, when we deny our need for help, instead of our weakness becoming strength, our strength becomes weakness. When we insist on building the illusion that we have it all under control, we barricade ourselves from the help we need.

Recently I tried to learn tennis as a hobby. I was pretty nervous when I went for my first lesson, and the first thing the instructor said didn't help. "All right, let's see what I've got to work with. What do you know?"

I told him I had no idea what I was doing. He said that was just the way he liked it, which confused me. He explained how people come all the time knowing just enough tennis to make them impossible to coach. They don't want to trust a new way because they are used to their way. And they try to show the coach how much they know instead of learning what he has to teach them.

"You're my favorite kind of person to work with," he said.

I wonder if God's favorite kind of person to work with is the one who says, "God, I have no idea what I'm doing here. But if you'll show me what you know about me, about life, about relationships, about my career, about my decisions, I'll do it."

Pride is the barrier that keeps us from receiving strength in our weakness. Sometimes you may find yourself embarrassed to ask others, or even God, for help. You may feel that you should be more mature by now, more capable. You know that God has called you to accomplish certain things, but the fact that your weaknesses keep getting in the way is humiliating. *Maybe God is running out of patience with me,* you think. *After all, I'm certainly out of patience with myself.*

God is not out of patience. And he probably has a significantly different assessment of yourself than you do.

Have you ever read the story of how God called a man named Gideon to rescue Israel from their oppressors, a country named Midian? It's found in Judges 6.

When God found Gideon, he wasn't doing heroic warrior things. He was hiding from the enemy. Despite that, God greeted Gideon with the optimistic phrase "The LORD is with you, mighty warrior" (verse 12).

Mighty warrior?

Understandably, Gideon reacted with a bit of sarcasm. "Oh really? If you are with us, then why do we hate our lives?" That's my paraphrase, in case you couldn't tell.

God ignored the sarcasm. "Go in the strength you have and save Israel out of Midian's hand. Am I not sending you?" (verse 14).

I love the phrase "the strength you have." God didn't expect Gideon to muster up superhero strength. He didn't scold him for his lack of courage, even though Gideon was hiding from his enemies in a wine press as God was speaking to him.

Gideon responded, slightly less sarcastically this time, "Pardon me, my lord, but how can I save Israel? My clan is the weakest in Manasseh, and I am the least in my family" (verse 15).

Gideon didn't try to hide his weakness from God. He was bluntly and blatantly honest. "I am weak. I am the least. I am not cut out for this. I have no idea what I'm doing." Those were his third words and thoughts. And God wasn't bothered in the least.

God replied, "I will be with you, and you will strike down all the Midianites, leaving none alive" (verse 16).

Is it just me, or does this sound like a sequel to Moses and the burning bush?

Over the next couple of chapters, God seemed determined to prove how little Gideon's weakness mattered. He even reduced the size of Gideon's army from thirty-two thousand to three hundred just to make the odds a little more interesting. Then God used those three hundred warriors to rout an innumerable, impossible army. Long before Hollywood and the Spartans came along, by the way.

Never once in this story does God appear frustrated with Gideon's lack of ability or manpower. We don't see God demanding that Gideon work out the details by himself, with his own logic and resources.

We see the opposite. In stages Gideon took on the courage and character of the God who called him. Gideon's excuses didn't change God's mind. God's empowerment eliminated Gideon's excuses.

In this story Gideon's claim to fame is not his leadership style, his motivational ability, or his military prowess, although each of these was eventually developed in Gideon's life. It's his faith, slow starting as it was. He was ultimately willing to believe and obey God.

That is what God wants from us as well. Not incredible strength. God already has that. He just wants us to have simple faith. To be willing to obey him because we believe him.

Centuries later another one of Israel's leaders learned the same thing. His name was Solomon. The night of Solomon's coronation God appeared to him and told him to ask for whatever he wanted. Talk about a genie-in-a-bottle experience.

Solomon's reply was incredibly honest.

> Now, LORD my God, you have made your servant king in place of my father David. But I am only a little child and do not know how to carry out my duties. Your servant is here among the people you have chosen, a great people, too numerous to count or number. So give your servant a discerning heart to govern your people and to distinguish between right and wrong. For who is able to govern this great people of yours? (1 Kings 3:7–9)

How did God respond? Did he reprimand Solomon for weak leadership? For calling himself "only a little child"? *Only* is not the kind of third word a king should have, after all. A king is supposed to have it all. Solomon should have told God his thirty-year long-range, strategic vision for Israel and then asked God to bless his plans for victory, for growth, and for success. That's what a real king would do, right?

The next verse gives us God's opinion of Solomon's honesty: "The Lord was pleased that Solomon had asked for this" (verse 10). God was delighted that Solomon knew his own limits and knew where to go for help. As a reward God didn't give Solomon just wisdom. He also gave him wealth, influence, and power.

Solomon had come face to face with his own lack of qualifications. But instead of hiding from those facts or being overwhelmed by them, he did exactly what he needed to do. He turned to God. He asked God to make up what was lacking.

And God did. In ways Solomon never could have imagined, much less have accomplished on his own.

God wants to do the same thing with our weaknesses. But in order to receive his help, we have to admit we need it. We have to take our weaknesses to God in faith, without self-condemnation or despair or shame.

Winning Through Weakness

The idea of winning through weakness probably seems anti-American. Maybe even antibiblical, depending on how you understand certain topics. The idea that our weaknesses could be good for us flies in the face of our self-help, DIY, never-take-no-for-an-answer culture. It almost sounds defeatist or pessimistic.

But it's not. It's the opposite.

I'm not advocating giving up. Rather, I'm saying we have to learn to make our weaknesses work for us. If we truly believe that God is in control of our lives, then we will look for the advantage in every attack. We will learn to perceive true strength in what seems to be weakness.

That was Joseph's conclusion in Genesis 50 after years—and several chapters—of roller-coaster circumstances. If anyone had the right to be jaded by the limitations and losses he had experienced, it was this guy. Having been kidnapped and trafficked into slavery by his own brothers, given up for dead by his father, falsely accused and unfairly jailed by his slave master, and forgotten by his friends, he found himself in a state of complete vulnerability. To the untrained eye, he was a prisoner of weakness.

But eventually, through a series of more fortunate events, he went from a prison to the palace, from total obscurity to near absolute authority.

From weakness to strength.

And when the brothers who betrayed him showed up to beg from him—oh, the irony—Joseph had the humility and maturity to realize what was going on.

He found the strength to do what must have appeared to be a weakness.

He wept with his brothers. He forgave his brothers.

And God used him to save his brothers.

His weakness became strength.

He didn't allow his strength to become his weakness.

Had Joseph never been in such a vulnerable and weak state, would he have had the compassion, the wisdom, and the opportunity to change world history and restore his family in the process?

Romans 8:28 says it this way: "We know that in all things God works for the good of those who love him, who have been called according to his purpose."

That promise has sustained Jesus's followers for millenniums, and it is as valid now as the day it was penned. We can expect our weaknesses to be used for God's glory and our benefit.

On a practical level how can weakness and strength coexist? How can weakness become strength, and how can God's strength be perfected in our weakness?

I don't claim to understand every nuance of God's dealings, so I'm not going to try to analyze and outline every possible way God could turn your weakness into strength. But here are a few thoughts that might help you see your failings in a more positive light.

First of all, if you never hurt, suffered, or struggled, how could you develop the strength you need to sustain the blessings God wants to bring into your life?

God also allows weakness in our lives to create a context that will showcase his strength. Paul said, "We have this treasure in jars of clay to show that this all-surpassing power is from God and not from us" (2 Corinthians 4:7).

God doesn't want the container to distract from the contents. So he uses our weakness as a contrast for his strength. It helps us remember that what's really valuable is what's inside. And what's inside comes from him, not us.

Also, whether we like it or not, our failures help keep us grounded, balanced, and healthy.

They are like governors. Not of the Arnold or Romney variety, of course. I'm talking about the speed-limiting devices installed on vehicles ranging from golf carts to mopeds to NASCAR. Vehicle manufacturers know enough about our love affair with adrenaline—and lawsuits—to realize they need to limit the maximum speeds of their machines. So they invented a device called a governor. Its sole function is to cut the gas supply just when things are getting exciting.

We can go too fast in life. We can get too much activity, too much responsibility, too many relationships, too much to manage, and even too much ministry. We can grow so quickly that we outstrip our ability to handle what we have.

And sooner or later we wreck the car and maybe hurt some people in the process.

I'm not saying God intentionally sabotages our advance, but I'm also not saying it's always the devil slowing us down. I'm convinced that God allows certain limitations because he knows what we're ready for and when we're ready. Limitations give us both time and motivation to grow into the opportunities he wants to provide.

When you read the biographies of world-changing men and women—whether it's Nelson Mandela or Steve Jobs—you find there's almost always an "exile" season. In other words, they experienced an apparent failure that ultimately enabled them to fulfill their purpose. The periods that seem the most unproductive often become most important. What's happening in us prepares us for what can and will happen to us and through us.

Rather than figuring out how to rewire the car and disable the governor, sometimes we just need to slow down. It's not as sexy. It's not as exhilarating. But it's sustainable and ultimately more effective.

I've been told that when you're learning golf, they tell you that if you want to hit the ball farther when you are teeing off, you have to slow down your swing.

That sounds counterproductive, and that kind of advice is exactly why you will never see me on a golf course.

But it can be good advice for our plans and goals. Slow your swing. Don't always try to crush every opportunity so fast and so far and so hard.

And although I don't play golf, I can hear my dad's voice in my head from when he coached me in my Little League baseball days. I would swing the bat so hard I'd lose sight of the ball, and he'd scream, "Stop trying to kill the ball! Just make contact!"

Instead of raging against our limits, we should learn to listen to them. To appreciate them. To let them guide our growth and inform our decisions. To keep our eye on the ball.

And just make contact.

Failing Closer

Our limitations and failures are also really good at keeping us connected to God. They help us draw closer to him. They remind us that we need him, that he is our source and our answer.

When things are going well in life, it's tempting to get distracted by our success and to think that is what life is all about. We start to chase after victory, prosperity, influence, and ministry.

There's nothing wrong with those things, but they were never meant to be the goal of life. They are meant to be the by-product of our growing relationship with Christ. In other words, they were meant to follow us as we chase after God.

Our limitations—far more than our abilities—remind us to return to our source of strength. They bring us back to God, back to dependency, back to relationship.

The biggest problem comes when we think that God is mad

at us for our mistakes. That he's disappointed because we dared to display frailty. That he's disgusted with our sins. Or that our weaknesses prove his displeasure with us.

If that's our view of God, then our weaknesses won't drive us toward him. They'll drive us away from him and into an existence dominated by condemnation, guilt, legalism, and maybe resentment. We'll end up striving to fix ourselves, to clean ourselves up, to make ourselves worthy of God. Or we'll give up on the process altogether because it's hopeless.

But as I've already pointed out, God is far less bothered by our weaknesses than we are. He knows what he's going to do about them. He even has plans to use them.

When we understand that, we can draw close to God. We can see him as a confidante, a Savior, and a co-conspirator of sorts. Even when we mess up. Even when we're embarrassed. Even when we're weak.

You've probably heard the adage "Fail forward." That means that when you fail, use it as an opportunity to learn and grow. Let your failures work for you.

Even more important, though, let your failures pull you closer to God. Fail closer—closer to God, closer to dependence, closer to faith.

Backstories Matter

Another benefit of weakness is that it helps us relate to others. Often our most heartfelt and authentic connections with other people are made through shared weaknesses.

What comfort would you have to offer someone who is going through personal pain if you had no frame of reference? Your trials give you credibility to say to someone who is hurting, "I have been there too, and we'll get through this together." True empathy is an empowering gift you can give only after you've gone through something that revealed your own weakness.

Whom do you listen to most when you need help? Intellectual know-it-alls? Or people who have walked the road you are on and lived to tell the story?

Often our greatest influence is birthed in our deepest suffering and brokenness. Our education, our eloquence, and our intelligence are helpful, but they aren't nearly as relatable as our weaknesses. We touch people around us because of the pain and humanity we share.

I realize that not everyone can or should be trusted with the details of our weaknesses. The goal isn't to parade our problems, wearing our weakness for the world to see. But as we learn to be vulnerable with God and with the right, trusted people, we discover that every weakness, properly processed, contains secret strength.

Think about the last time you broke down and cried in front of a friend. It might have felt uncomfortable. It might have embarrassed you. But I bet that moment of vulnerability did more to win the person's heart and cement your friendship than any other experience you've shared.

There is something about weakness that opens hearts. It disarms the defensive. It softens the suspicious. It endears the indifferent.

It shows people that we aren't to be feared or revered. We are "one of them," and as such, we are welcome to speak into their lives.

I heard someone say that the two words people need to hear the most when they're hurting are not *you should* but *me too.*

Case in point: Jesus. He made his grand entrance into the human race as a baby. That says a lot right there. Human infants are about the most helpless creatures on the planet.

On top of that his mom was an unwed teenager. His dad was a working-class dude. They were from Nazareth, a backwater town that was known for being the butt of jokes. Jesus's upbringing could not have been further from what royalty—much less divinity—would have expected.

Then, after thirty years of unrecorded humanity, he started his ministry, which lasted only three and a half years.

If you do the math, more than 85 percent of his life was spent in obscurity.

The Bible makes a point of showing Jesus's human weaknesses throughout his ministry. Jesus lived without sin, of course, but he experienced fatigue, hunger, thirst, anger, sadness, tragedy, betrayal, criticism, temptation, persecution, and ultimately death.

What's with the backstory? Have you ever wondered? Was it really necessary for him to go through infancy and potty training and puberty? Did he have to walk this planet and suffer its ails for so long? Why didn't he show up like Thor, a muscle-bound superhero descending from the sky to save humanity?

Hebrews tells us why Jesus was so . . . weak.

> We do not have a high priest who is unable to empathize with our weaknesses, but we have one who has been tempted in every way, just as we are—yet he did not sin. Let us then approach God's throne of grace with confidence, so that we may receive mercy and find grace to help us in our time of need. (4:15–16)

In other words, while Jesus's righteousness saves us, his humanity is what draws us near to him. That's what bridges the gap between God and man.

The person of Jesus is God's resounding "Me too!"

The apostle Paul put it perfectly:

> For to be sure, he was crucified in weakness, yet he lives by God's power. Likewise, we are weak in him, yet by God's power we will live with him in our dealing with you. (2 Corinthians 13:4)

In Jesus, our weakness is heaven's secret weapon.

8

Changing Change

When Holly and I had our first child, Elijah, I had a lot to learn.

Understatement alert.

I had *everything* to learn.

I remember during the pregnancy I had so many fears. *What if something goes wrong? Is she allowed to eat that? Will breathing smog provoke a spontaneous sex change in the womb? Somebody's smoking a cigarette. Can I make a citizen's arrest?* I had a never-ending litany of concerns, worries, and unknowns.

Right after the birth one of the nurses started talking about something called an Apgar test.

Test? I didn't know there was going to be a test. The kid just saw daylight for the first time, and he already had to take a test?

They explained there was a scale, and they rated him based on his color and heart rate and all that.

I said, "How did he do? Did he win?"

They said, "Mr. Furtick, your baby is healthy."

My immediate feeling was mission accomplished!

I still remember that sense of relief. *Now I don't have to worry about the baby anymore. We did it. By that I mean Holly did it. But the main thing is, we don't have to worry anymore.*

I didn't know that what I thought was the closing ceremony was just the starting gun. That I was about to enter a new reality of diaper disasters and stroller emergencies and sleep deprivation and endless opportunities for panic.

We took Elijah home. After a few days we went on a walk around the neighborhood. I noticed bugs were flying around his head. I panicked. I tucked him under my arm like a football and ran for the house, because no insects were going to land on my baby boy. Holly was laughing, but I didn't care. I wasn't going to let my kid get West Nile virus.

Keep in mind, Elijah was our first child. We have three now. By the third one, things were different. "Abbey, they're just bugs. Go ahead. Play with them, swallow them. I'm sure they're a good source of protein."

But when it's your first child, needless anxiety is part of the package I suppose.

A few days after the kamikaze bug episode, we were at home. Elijah was in his crib, and he was supposed to be falling asleep, but instead he was screaming. That was his general pattern for the first year of life, by the way. We could hear it through the baby monitor. But we let things continue for a few minutes to see if he would conk out on his own.

Then the monitor crackled a bit, and the screaming stopped. At first I was relieved there was silence, but then worry flooded in. *Did he fall asleep? Or did he die? Maybe he's choking. Maybe he's in trouble and can't say anything, and I'm just sitting here enjoying the silence.*

I remember running into the room and flinging open the door.

He was sound asleep, of course, or at least he was until I barged in.

Afterward I said to Holly, "I had this stupid male idea of childbirth, that once the baby was born, we would stop worrying. But I'm getting the feeling that this is just the beginning of a lifetime."

Holly said something very profound. "Yeah, I guess trusting God with the lives of your children is a lifelong process, and it only gets more challenging with time."

I knew it was true. Sure, I can protect my kids from bugs right now. But eventually they will grow up and go off to college. I won't be able to tuck them under my arm and save them from dumb roommates or unsafe drivers.

I've learned something. It's easy to get married and dream about having kids. But "having kids" is not a goal that you check off your bucket list. It's not some achievement or accomplishment that you finish, and then you pat yourself on the back and move on.

"Having kids" is not an event, not a project. It's a process.

The process of having children tells us a lot about the nature of God. Think about it. What is the point of toddlers? Why did he dream up teenagers? Just imagine how far ahead civilization would be if we didn't spend the first eighteen years of our lives dealing with potty training and pimples and puberty and proms.

God could have created us as fully formed humans. We could have started somewhere around forty years old. That seems like a nice spot, don't you think? We would have some wisdom, but we wouldn't have arthritis.

But instead, he put us in the world in a state of complete dependency. Why? Because he's a God of process.

The same holds true for our spiritual walk. When we put our faith in Jesus, that wasn't the closing ceremony. It wasn't the finish line. It didn't mean that from that moment on we would think, walk, talk, and act exactly like Jesus. That may sound obvious, but I've met a lot of people who expect to come out of the phone booth with an *S* on their chests following their salvation experience.

Two of my favorite Bible verses are Colossians 2:6–7: "So then, just as you received Christ Jesus as Lord, continue to live your lives in him, rooted and built up in him, strengthened in the faith as you were taught, and overflowing with thankfulness."

In other words, we received Jesus at a particular point in time. But that wasn't the end of the story. Now we need to continue in him. Live in him. Be rooted and built up in him. Be strengthened in our faith in him.

Sometimes we worry because we don't seem to be changing fast enough. We look at the failures and weaknesses that plague us, and we get frustrated. Why can't we get better faster? Wouldn't we be more useful to God? Wouldn't we be more qualified to follow him and serve him?

But when it comes to fixing us, God has his own timetable.

Project or Process

That's hard for us to hear, because we are a project-oriented culture. We love goals, we love resolutions, and we love results. There's nothing wrong with that, necessarily.

I live for the thrill of getting stuff done. It's almost a high for me to check something off a list. In fact, sometimes when I complete a task I didn't plan on doing, I'll go back and put it on my list, even though it's already completed, just so I can get the rush of checking it off. What? Doesn't everybody do that?

This has worked for me and against me throughout my life. At times it's enabled me to push through to completion, because I'm a finisher. But at other times, when I'm considering starting something that's going to take a while, or when I'm in the middle of something and see no end in sight, I freeze up. If I can't assign a time line to it and see significant progress along the way, I lose motivation pretty quickly.

Throughout this book we've been discussing our identities. We've been looking at our third words, at our weaknesses and strengths, at the oxymoronic dichotomy of accepting who we are right now while becoming who God means for us to become.

There's a word for all that: *process.*

The Christian walk is not a finish line. It's not a goal or an achievement. It's an ongoing relationship with Jesus. It's a progression of growing and changing, of embracing and replacing, of listening to God's voice and living out who he says we are.

It's a process, and it will last the rest of our lives.

Following Jesus is an ongoing, ever-evolving experience. And the sooner we realize that and accept it, the more we'll enjoy the journey.

Change Is Overrated

It's easy enough to say we need to be patient with the process. To talk about the benefits of weaknesses. To extol the virtues of embracing who we really are.

But I think we all know why we are in such a hurry to change.

Because mistakes *hurt.* They are painful, embarrassing, and messy.

That's the nature of mistakes, and I think that's the number-one motivator for change.

And I know, spiritually speaking, our motivation for change should be to please God.

On an idealistic level, that is true. That is noble. And if that's how you live, you are incredible. I applaud you.

But if we are honest, most of us don't change until we have to. Until our frustration with the way things are reaches a boiling point. Until none of the pants in our closet fit. Until we've run ourselves so ragged that we're paying the price in our health and relationships. Or until our issues have created enough isolation to bring us back to ourselves. It's called *learning the hard way,* and it's a universal human pattern.

Sometimes we interpret the pain of our mistakes as punishment from God. I don't see it that way. I think the pain of our mistakes can actually be a gift to help us realize our potential for change.

Why do you think God wants us to make those changes in the first place? It's more about us than about him. And while it's true that God wants us to glorify him and reflect him accurately, he isn't a capricious despot. He doesn't need us to measure up to a standard of perfection in order to feel good about himself as God.

God knows certain things will suck the life out of us. They will hurt us. They will hurt people around us. They will hurt our relationship with him.

So he calls them sin, and he enables us to stop doing them.

Let's get this straight. God doesn't ask us to change because it adds anything to him. It's not for his benefit that we get our lives together.

It's for ours. The obedience and holiness he asks from us are for our well-being and the well-being of those around us.

I think we can all agree that sin confuses and complicates our lives. It causes us to lose ground, lose face, and lose out. Mistakes are, by our definition anyway, bad.

No wonder we try so hard to reverse and eliminate them. We make New Year's resolutions. We join a CrossFit box. We go back to school. We watch TED Talks.

We are convinced that a failure-free existence is just around the corner. If we want it bad enough, if we try hard enough, if we study diligently enough, if we strain and strive and push long enough, we will arrive. We will overcome our weaknesses, and we will finally be happy.

But that never happens.

I don't mean we never improve. Of course we do. That's one of the perks of being human. We have a massive amount of control over who we become and what we accomplish. We just never arrive as we think we will. We strive and make progress, and that is briefly rewarding, but then there is more work to be done.

And often our improvements don't make us as happy as we hoped.

Ironically, the more we fix ourselves, the more we become aware of how much we still have left to fix. It's the paradox of perfection. Paradise seems so close, yet it always stays on the horizon, tempting and taunting us. So we sell out to self-improvement, and years down the road we wonder why we still aren't happy.

Yes, we should strive to be the best possible version of ourselves. But we need to realize that self-improvement in and of itself doesn't produce happiness. Fewer failures don't always equate with a more satisfied life.

Why? Because our weaknesses are not necessarily the source of our unhappiness. Therefore, perfection is not the cure.

Change is good. Change is necessary. Change is inevitable.

But change for the sake of change is overrated.

I'm Not Flossing

It's overrated because there is more to life than self-help and self-improvement. There is something far more profound, permanent, and fulfilling.

That *something* is discovering new dimensions in our relationship with God. It's not necessarily something you can check off a list. But that's what gives everything on the list meaning to begin with. Our relationship with God must not become primarily a means to get to our goals. When our priorities are right, our goals become a means to grow closer to God. And whether we are hitting all our goals or not, if we are learning to rely on God more, we are accomplishing the ultimate goal.

Knowing Jesus is the only thing that can complete us and satisfy us. We were created with a need to know God, and when we turn to him, we find the source of lasting fulfillment.

Change is temporarily gratifying, but relationship is perpetually satisfying.

That's the point of the process. To be with him. To "continue to live . . . in him," as Colossians 2:6 says.

We can't reduce Christianity to a self-help program. Jesus didn't bleed and die on the cross so we could perfect ourselves. He didn't take our sins upon himself so we could sit around and critique each other into perfection.

Have you ever seen monkeys at a zoo picking bugs from each other's fur? It's gross and tender at the same time. Mostly gross.

Sometimes we do the same as Jesus's followers. We think it is our God-given calling and the height of Christian charity to nitpick at each other and ourselves. To get out our magnifying glasses and tweezers and try to eliminate every last trace of our sinful nature.

Meanwhile, a world around us is in desperate need of the love and grace of God. People are hungry for what we have, but we're too discouraged by our first-world sins—our temper problems and our pride issues and our pornography addictions—to notice. We think we have to be perfect before we can be effective.

But that won't happen on this planet. And if it did, we'd probably be insufferably arrogant. And completely unrelatable.

We are in the same process as every saint and sinner out there. That's okay. It's even helpful. Let God use you no matter where you find yourself in that process.

Please don't misunderstand me. I've said this time and time again: I'm not excusing sin. We should be on a continual quest both to better ourselves and to be a blessing to others.

But self-perfection is not the goal of human existence.

Relationship with God is. Walking with God is. Knowing God, following God, listening to God, obeying God—those are the things humanity was made for.

Not picking nits from each other's fur or specks from each other's eyes—or our own.

When we get to heaven, sin will no longer be an issue. But our relationship with God will continue for eternity. That should tell us something: we shouldn't lose sight of what is eternal in our efforts to improve what is temporary.

I realize what I am saying could sound scary, because as Christians we spend an inordinate amount of time examining our faults and attempting to fix them. We might think that if we relax our death grip on holiness, we'll fall into the clutches of sin.

But the longer I follow Jesus, the more I realize that his dealings in our lives are far more secure than that. He is the author and finisher. He is the one who gives us both the will and the way to obey. He takes the initiative. He takes the lead. He provides the power to change.

God has a timetable for our lives, and chances are, it is different from ours. Maybe the third words that drive us crazy aren't as high on his priority list as they are on ours. So we think we aren't changing, because we don't see our top ten improving very quickly.

But at any given moment, we are experiencing profound change—often without even noticing it. Eventually we'll look back and realize that God has been doing amazing things all along.

The reason I'm so passionate about having a realistic view of change is because the opposite—thinking we have to fix everything perfectly and right now—is counterproductive and depressing. It creates cynicism and hopelessness, and as a result it undermines the goals it attempts to reach.

I went to a new dentist recently.

When the dental hygienist met with me, I said, "I need you to understand something straight out and up front. I'm going to be the worst patient you've ever had in your life because I'm not doing anything you tell me to do between now and the next time I come in."

She sort of laughed. But I wasn't joking.

"I'll be back in six months," I continued, "but in the meantime I'm not flossing. I have a retainer on the back of my teeth, and I'm not threading that little plastic string down in there. I tried it, and it's annoying. So you can give me floss, but it's going to end up in the trash can. I'm probably not even going to take it out of this office. I'll put it in the trash can in the lobby.

"And while we're being honest, I'm not brushing three times a day. I'll brush at least once, and twice on a good day. But that's the best you're going to get.

"I know I need a mouth guard, because I bite down on my

teeth at night. I know I'm not going to have any teeth by age forty. But I put that mouth guard in the last time they gave me one, and it choked me. I'm not into choking at night, so you might as well save the mouth guard. I'm not using it."

That poor lady. She should charge extra for people like me.

As a pastor, sometimes I get stares from people in the audience that remind me of my attitude toward the dentist.

"I've tried that. Didn't work for me. I'll listen to you, but I'm not going to do anything you say."

I get that. I really do. Whether it's our dental-hygiene habits or our walk with God, we have all run into the same issue. *We tried that.*

We tried to change. We tried to do better. We had great hopes and expectations and faith that things were going to improve.

But they didn't, and now we are a bit cynical. How do we stay committed to the process when the process doesn't seem to be going anywhere?

Keep Circling

When I gave my life to Christ at age sixteen, I thought it was a project that was completed. I read that Jesus said on the cross, "It is finished" (John 19:30). I saw that Paul wrote, "If anyone is in Christ, he is a new creation" (2 Corinthians 5:17, NKJV).

So I thought, *Cool. From now on, when I see a pretty girl, I won't have any lustful, tempting thoughts about her.*

Then a cheerleader walked by me. I hadn't been a child of God for twenty-four hours yet, and *boom.* Same feeling.

Only now I knew it was wrong. Now I felt bad about it. But it was still there. And I couldn't understand why. It was depressing.

I'm sure you've felt this frustration, maybe on a much more sophisticated level. For example, maybe you read in Ephesians 5 how you need to love your wife more. You think, *Okay. I need to love my wife as Christ loved the church.* So you go home and you wash the dishes.

She seems unimpressed. She doesn't even say, "Thank you." She doesn't make love to you right there in the kitchen.

So you think, *I tried that. I did that love thing I heard about. It didn't work.*

Remember, it's a process. If you've been zoning out for months, staring at your phone every night after dinner, washing the dishes one time probably won't undo all of that.

Or how about this one? Someone hurt you once, and you thought you had forgiven him. But then you hear he got a promotion at work, and you find yourself vaguely upset. And it makes you realize that deep inside you secretly still hoped he'd have to pay for what he did to you. It wasn't like you wanted him to die in a car wreck or anything, but you definitely didn't want him to climb the ladder of success.

It's discouraging. *I thought I was over that,* you think in dismay. *I thought I was bigger than that.*

Walking with God is usually not a straight line from here to there. It's a process that can be a little disorienting sometimes. And if we don't understand the time element involved, if we don't have right expectations, we can end up disillusioned and defeated.

In churchspeak, we tend to look at the word *salvation* as past tense. We say things like "I was saved when I was sixteen." Or "I've been saved for twenty years."

We treat it as if it were an event, but in reality it's a process. The Bible talks about salvation in all three primary tenses: past, present, and future.

When we put our faith in Jesus, we *were* saved. "For it is by grace you have been saved, through faith" (Ephesians 2:8). That's past tense. It's done. It's accomplished. And it happened in a moment.

But we are also *being* saved. Present tense. "For the message of the cross is foolishness to those who are perishing, but to us who are being saved it is the power of God" (1 Corinthians 1:18). That speaks about the process of change, of growth, of depth.

And then there's a future element to salvation. We *will be* saved. "This inheritance is kept in heaven for you, who through faith are shielded by God's power until the coming of the salvation that is ready to be revealed in the last time" (1 Peter 1:4–5).

We *were* saved, we *are being* saved, we *will be* saved. There's no doubt about it. Walking with God is a lifelong experience. And beyond.

Yes, we are already forgiven. We'll never be more forgiven than we are right now. We'll never be more loved than we are right now. We've already arrived, and we're already accepted. But at the same time, it's going to be a process, because we are being changed and transformed each day. And the process will not be complete until we see Christ face to face, when he makes us just like he is.

I don't know about you, but I have a lot of stuff to process.

Some of it happened before I was ever born, and it's in my genes. Some of it has to do with my own decisions, with habits that grew to have a hold on me.

And I get very tired of circling around the same issues. I've prayed about them. I've thought I had victory over them. So it's frustrating to find myself doing laps around the same issues over and over. And that frustration fills me with a sense of low-grade hopelessness. One of my favorite nineties bands, Extreme, had an underrated song titled "Am I Ever Gonna Change?" I remember thinking even as a teenager that the title of that song was the defining question of my life. As an adult, I have found the question even more exasperating.

I was talking to a friend recently about one issue that I've dealt with my whole life: my temper. I'm not violent or belligerent, but I can be a bit of a jerk. I can be quite irritable and snappy with the people I love most, even moments after preaching.

So I was explaining to my friend, who is also a professional counselor, that I was *sick of myself.*

He responded, "Why would you say something like that?"

"Because I keep struggling with the same thing. I'm tired of circling this thing over and over. With all the knowledge I have and considering how good God has been to me, I should be over this."

I wasn't mad at God. I was mad at myself. I was looking at myself and thinking, *After all God has given me, why can't I change? Here I go. Another lap around the temper-tantrum pool. It started when I was born. It won't be over until I die.*

When I told my friend, "I'm tired of circling this," he said mysteriously, "Well, at least you're not circling it at the same level anymore."

Total counselor move.

He went on to say, "I've been your friend for years now. Yeah, you still struggle with the same stuff, but I've noticed you don't talk about it at the same level anymore. Now you talk about it from the heart. You used to be all about your behaviors and outcomes. Now you talk about your motivations. It's a deeper level."

Let me ask you. Is it possible that even though you're circling the same issue, God is working in your heart at a deeper level? Maybe you have more reason to celebrate than you realize.

My friend wasn't done, though. "Another thing," he said. "I see you circling this issue, but you're at a higher altitude."

"Wait a minute, am I circling deeper or higher?" I was confused by what struck me as a mixed metaphor.

He went on, unfazed. "You have more awareness. You're mentioning things now that you didn't even know you dealt with a couple of years ago when I met you. You're changing a lot even though the struggle feels just as strong as ever."

Just because I am circling the same issue doesn't mean I'm stuck on the same level. Recognizing this has been a game changer for me. I hope it speaks to you as well.

Maybe you've been beating yourself up inside lately, thinking, *Why am I so impossible? Why can't I get it together?*

Maybe your change just hasn't surfaced yet. That doesn't mean it's not happening. And some of what seems like pointless circling around the same challenge may be practice for the victory lap to come.

THE FINISHER

Finish what you start. It's a popular mantra.

But when it comes to our walk with God, we didn't start this in the first place. God did.

If it had been up to us to start things, we would still be far from God. But God drew near. He sent his Son. "While we were still sinners, Christ died for us" (Romans 5:8). God stepped into the middle of our chaos and disobedience, our running and roaming and denying the very One who made us. He interrupted the cycle and said, "My grace is sufficient" (2 Corinthians 12:9).

Earlier I quoted Colossians 2:6. "So then, just as you received Christ Jesus as Lord, continue to live your lives in him." Notice how it ends.

If you read that as a command to live for God, you're not reading it right. It doesn't say live *for* him. It says live *in* him.

It's an invitation. God isn't saying, "If you claim to know Jesus, you'd better live like him." He's saying, "If you know Jesus, you *get* to live *with* him." It's a privilege and a relationship.

Our struggles don't necessarily mean we are distant from God. Sometimes when we are struggling the most, we are actually closest to him. We are more aware than ever of our desperate need for him, and he responds with grace and patience.

This is not about a destination. It's about a journey. And the same grace that got us into this relationship is the grace that is going to carry us through.

The verse ends with the phrase "in him." It doesn't say *in it*; it says *in him.* The Christian life is not an it. It's a him. It's not a principle or a program. It's a person. It's Jesus.

The next time you find yourself circling the same sin, remember Jesus. When you feel as if you're taking a lap around your laziness, wondering, *Why can't I be more disciplined?* Or the next time you are taking a lap around your spending dysfunction, thinking, *Why can't I be more frugal?* Or the next time you're taking a lap around your inability to stick with anything longer than a couple of weeks or your inability to be patient with people who get on your nerves or your inability to produce under pressure.

Remember Jesus.

The end of yourself is often the beginning of grace. Turn your eyes on Jesus, and let him take the lead. He's even more interested in your transformation than you are. He's more patient with you than you are. He's committed to the process, and he'll lead you each step of the way.

The author of Hebrews wrote this:

> Therefore, since we are surrounded by such a great cloud of witnesses, let us throw off everything that hinders and the sin that so easily entangles. And let us run with perseverance the race marked out for us, fixing our eyes on Jesus, the pioneer and perfecter of faith. (12:1–2)

How will we finish the race? By looking at Jesus. He is the pioneer and initiator of our faith, and he is the perfecter and finisher.

I realize this can sound a little abstract. But really, it's as simple as focus. If your thoughts are on how far you have to go, your steps will feel heavy and uncertain. But if your focus is on how far God has already brought you, and if your confidence is in what Jesus has already done for you, the energy to endure will be yours.

"Finish what you started," the world says. But God says the opposite: "Just continue what I've already finished. Enjoy what I've already won."

Jesus died for you, and he rose for you, and he declared that you are forgiven and free. Keep walking. Do another lap. He's teaching you. You are growing. You are getting closer to him.

You're not perfect yet, but you're in a process, and that's what matters most.

What I find profoundly encouraging is that when it comes to the fathers of our faith, the Bible doesn't shy away from the process. God doesn't attempt to hide their humanity or paint over their problems.

Their mistakes are forever recorded, not just as a warning, but even more so as an encouragement. If they could do it, so can we.

We've mentioned a few of them already: Moses, Joseph, Gideon, David, Solomon, Paul—even Jesus. They all faced weaknesses and limitations. Despite that, God accomplished great things in and through them.

But if I had to pick one character out of the entire biblical gallery that epitomizes this idea of process, of weakness and growth, of wrong third words and right third words, I know exactly which person I'd pick.

In all his complexities this guy was certainly familiar with process. He was part hero and part villain, part aggressor and part victim. He spent his life trying to get everything the wrong way and at the wrong time until he finally learned to embrace himself and the process he was in.

His name is Jacob. And his life was colorful, incontrovertible proof that God loves to work with unqualified and even disqualified people.

THE GOD OF JACOB

The two figures silhouetted against the rising sun were a curious sight. Or at least they would have been if anyone had been watching. They had wrestled for hours, but neither would give in.

Nearby a campsite was abandoned and silent. Clearly it had been vacated in a hurry. A few coals, some discarded scraps of equipment, and a sense of fear were all that remained.

The men struggled and fought as if their lives depended on it.

And for one of them, it did.

The Power of Crisco

I've created my fair share of imaginary identities. Not because I aim to deceive. Maybe because I long to belong. Or maybe because embracing who I really am is just too uncomfortable. It's probably a bit of both.

I remember as a six-year-old running around my backyard every afternoon yelling, "By the power of Crisco! I have the power!" And I would raise my plastic He-Man Power Sword in the air and imagine Crisco's power—whatever that was—transforming me into a superhero.

I vaguely remember my mom laughing in the kitchen and my neighbor, Mr. Buddy, smiling as he puttered with his lawn mower. I couldn't figure out what was so amusing.

Then one day my mom had to tell me the hard truth. Or in this case, the greasy truth.

"Honey, do you know what Crisco is?"

"Yes ma'am, it's what He-Man uses to get his superpowers."

"It is?"

"Yes ma'am! Prince Adam raises his sword and says, 'By the

power of Crisco!' and he turns into He-Man, and then he says, 'I have the power!' and he points his sword at Cringer and turns him into Battle Cat."

Then my mom told me what Crisco really was. She even showed me a can. She told me that my favorite superhero was actually calling on the power of Grayskull.

Crisco . . . Grayskull. Tomato, to-mah-to.

She said, "But you can call it the power of Crisco if you want, baby. It's cute."

"I don't want to. I'll sound stupid."

That was the last time I raised the Power Sword.

But not the last time I pretended I was more powerful than I really was, nor the last time I tried to get my power from the wrong source.

Grownups may have more sophisticated rituals than children, but our proficiency at pretending to be anyone but ourselves is remarkable—and not in a good way. To quote the inimitable Prince, "All of our life's a stage, everybody's stars, reality's so blurry."[9]

Have you ever thought about how much of our lives revolves around appearance, image, reputation, and recognition? We launch daily personal PR campaigns to prove, if only to ourselves, that we are competent and valuable.

We are all too familiar with our shortcomings and weaknesses. They embarrass us, frustrate us, and mock us. So eventually we conclude that getting ahead in life will require us to become more like someone else.

And we learn to fake it till we make it or until the faking breaks us, whichever comes first.

Jacob, our case study for the next few chapters, was a master pretender. What did that get him? Where did it land him?

Just Jacob

Jacob had identity issues from the moment he was born. The poor guy was set up for failure.

Even the name Jacob is less than positive. It literally means "heel grabber." That sounds bizarre, but it wasn't a case of his parents not looking up the meaning of the name in a baby book before they filled out the birth certificate. And it's not quite as bad as Clem or La–a. Actually his name was intentional. Maybe you've read the story, which is found in Genesis 25.

Jacob was a twin. He and his brother, Esau, were ridiculously competitive. They even fought in the womb. And when it came time to be born, Esau came out first but just barely. Jacob was holding on to Esau's heel.

Hence the name.

In our culture that would have been nothing more than a story to laugh about later. Maybe bragging rights for Esau. But back then birth order was everything.

As the firstborn, Esau had two unique privileges: the birthright and the blessing. The first meant he received double the inheritance. Their father, Isaac, was beyond wealthy, so that was quite a chunk of change.

But even more important was the blessing. That referred to God's hand of prosperity and multiplication for the rest of his life. It referred to a transfer of authority and leadership in the family from the father to the son.

Jacob apparently never got over losing the race down the birth canal. He spent the next few decades plotting and scheming to get what Esau had.

His third word was *Jacob,* and he didn't like what that meant. He wanted to be Esau—or at least to have what Esau had. But he was just Jacob, and to be Jacob seemed second best.

The Bible takes time to point out that, despite being twins, Esau and Jacob were polar opposites. When Esau was born, he was red and hairy. I'll withhold my comments about how his parents must have felt when one of their long-awaited sons came out looking like baby Chewbacca. Esau grew up to be an outdoorsman and a hunter. He was tough. He was rough. He could skin a buck and run a trotline. The star of the original *Duck Dynasty.*

But Jacob? The Bible says he was a smooth-skinned, quiet man who liked to stay among the tents. Translated, he may have been a mama's boy. He may have been more into HGTV than ESPN.

To top it off, their parents played favorites. Their father, Isaac, loved Esau, but their mother, Rebekah, loved Jacob.

Jacob grew up in the shadow of his brother. Esau was always bigger, faster, and better. The external differences must have only highlighted the fact that Jacob was never quite enough. *If I had just been born a few minutes earlier,* Jacob probably thought, *security and blessing would have been mine.*

Interestingly, the name Jacob doesn't just mean "heel grabber." It also means "deceiver, supplanter, or usurper." It refers to a person who pretends to be somebody or something in order to take what isn't his.

Jacob's parents couldn't have picked a more appropriate name. Jacob wanted Esau's position so badly that he tricked him into giving up his birthright in exchange for a bowl of soup. I'll talk more about that in the next chapter.

But the biggest trick of all came later in their lives when Isaac was about to die.

Playing Favorites

At this point Isaac was so old that he couldn't see. He knew he didn't have much time left, and he wanted to give Esau the blessing. So Isaac called Esau and told him to hunt some game and bring him food, and then he would bless him.

Enter Rebekah, the boys' mother. After hearing all this from the other room, she called Jacob. She told him (loosely paraphrased), "This is your chance to get the blessing you've been chasing since you were born. Esau is out hunting, but he'll be back soon, so we'll have to make this quick. I'll cook some food and dress you up in Esau's clothes. We'll even put animal skins on your neck and arms in case Isaac touches you. Trust me, your dad's too blind to know the difference. By the time Esau gets back, his blessing will be yours. And there will be nothing he can do about it."

Before we continue with the story, we have to recognize

something. I believe it's a pivotal point in the narrative, and it goes a long way toward explaining why Esau and Jacob turned out the way they did.

Because Isaac and Rebekah played favorites, Esau and Jacob grew up in an environment where at any given moment at least one parent didn't think they were good enough. They were compared to each other, contrasted with each other, and set against each other.

No wonder the twins turned out to be dysfunctional.

This makes me wonder: How many of our identity issues and our third words were set in place by our early-life experiences? I'm no psychologist, but the questions are worth asking.

Why am I pretending? Why am I trying to be someone else? Who told me who I should be? And why do I feel as though I can never measure up?

Had Isaac been more affirming of Jacob's differences, would Jacob have felt the need to masquerade as Esau? Had their parents loved them both the same, would the boys have grown up valuing each other's strengths and weaknesses rather than competing and conniving to tear each other down?

I can tell you that in my life, both as a child and now as a parent of three kids, I have witnessed the weight that parents' third words carry in the lives of their children. It's exciting and sobering at the same time.

Parents can propel their kids into becoming who they were meant to be, or parents can subtly drive their children to pretend, posture, and pose because they think that who they are is not good enough.

If you are a parent, you have the awesome responsibility of helping your children realize who they are. You have a God-given insight into their identities, and you get to play a part in bringing those identities to light.

This doesn't mean you control them or force them to conform to your ideas for their lives. This isn't about making them miniversions of you. It isn't about living vicariously through them, pushing them to fulfill the dreams you never accomplished and quarterbacking teams you never got to play on.

This is about valuing who they are right now, in whatever stage of life and maturity they happen to be. It's about seeing with eyes of faith the incredible people they are right now and watering the seeds of what they can become.

Most important, it's about helping *them* value and recognize who they are.

This isn't always easy, as any parent of a junior high student can attest. Suddenly their peers, both friends and bullies, start suggesting some new third words, and as parents we have the task of helping them sort through it all.

My kids are still young, but already I can see glimpses of who they are and who they will become. I can't wait to watch their journeys of self-discovery and self-realization. To see the lights come on in their eyes as they realize they are valuable and capable and called. To hear them share dreams that God himself has dropped into their hearts.

Most of us can think back to our childhood and identify moments when certain third words were given to us. Words that we believed. Words that shaped who we became and how we lived from then on. Maybe we can remember when we started to suspect that we weren't good enough, that we didn't measure up to the expectations and demands of those in authority over us.

So we started to pretend. We built facades, we concocted identities, we tried to bury the real us in order to be more pleasing to those whose opinions we valued.

Again, I'm not a psychologist. My goal isn't to analyze you or categorize you. And identity is a complicated thing, as we saw earlier. But the complications of our identity aren't intimidating to God.

If you grew up in a dysfunctional environment, if you were a victim of identity abuse, comparison, manipulation, or favoritism, know that God longs to reveal the true you. The you that has deep value. The you that you are called to be. And the you that has been freed to grow into that calling. Ask him to show you if you have adopted personas and pretenses that are harming you.

I'm not saying we are the inevitable products of other people's definitions of us. We all choose our paths. We can't blame who we are or what we've done on everyone else.

But the value systems we absorbed as children are powerful. They have shaped us, labeled us, and at times limited us, and often we don't even realize it.

So again, ask yourself, *Why am I pretending?*

It might be time to let go of some unhealthy concepts of your identity and worth that you've held on to since childhood. It might be time to believe that you really are better than *they* said . . . whoever *they* might be. That you are stronger. That you are more capable. That you are more valuable.

It might be time to figure out who you really are and to value the real you as much as God does.

The Pretender

When Rebekah told Jacob her grand scheme, Jacob wasn't so sure. But he went along with it. I used to feel sorry for Jacob. His mom talked him into scamming his brother, and he ended up suffering the consequences. What I didn't realize until studying this a bit further was that, at this point, Jacob was seventy-six years old. At seventy-six it's a little late to blame your mom, buddy. You have to take ownership of your life.

Genesis 27 describes how Rebekah and Jacob executed their elaborate plot to get the blessing. At first Isaac was suspicious because he thought he recognized Jacob's voice. But when he felt the hairy skin and smelled the aroma of the fields, he was convinced. The pretense worked. Isaac blessed Jacob.

Right about then Esau showed up. When he found out what Jacob had done, he didn't just become angry. He became murderous. He started breathing fire and obscenities and threats, and everyone knew he was serious. And everyone knew he was good with weapons.

Which left only one option for his younger brother, who was good in the kitchen.

Run, Jacob, run!

Jacob got the blessing, but he spent the next twenty-one years as a fugitive, exiled from home and family and country.

Some blessing.

But that is what happens when we try to get God to bless someone we are not.

I said it earlier: *God can't bless who you pretend to be.* In the appearance-driven, comparison-crazed culture we live in, that's a truth we need to take to heart.

Jacob was a pretender. He knew how to scheme and scam. He had become skilled at conning and conniving. He could dress, act, and talk the part to get what he wanted.

But when he got the blessing of Isaac he so desperately wanted, it came with unexpected baggage. He found himself alone, afraid, and on the run.

Yes, Jacob eventually received material blessings, as we read later in the story. So on that level, his ruse worked.

But did it satisfy him as he'd hoped? I doubt he counted on fleeing for his life from a homicidal sibling.

Hundreds of years later Solomon wrote: "The blessing of the LORD makes a person rich, and he adds no sorrow with it" (Proverbs 10:22, NLT).

In other words, when God gives us something, he also gives us the ability to enjoy it. That doesn't mean we suddenly have perfect, pain-free lives. But it means that we find true fulfillment and satisfaction when we get his blessings, his way, in his time.

The blessing Jacob received was limited as long as he was dressed like Esau. And it is the same for you and me when we live as if we were someone else.

If we're honest, it's easy to relate to Jacob. At one time or another, we've all worn the costume. We've all talked and acted and dressed like He-Man, knowing deep down the power of Crisco isn't cutting it. Then we wonder why life feels empty, why things never change, and why we're disappointed in ourselves at the deepest level.

Three Different Me's

For me personally, part of the problem is that there are *at least* three versions of me. First, there's the me I currently am. This guy has an upside, but he also has plenty of weaknesses and issues. Most of them have been there for years. He's inconsistent, often boring, and sometimes even disappointing. I call him *Frustrating Furtick.*

Then there is the me I *wish* I could be. This guy is the opposite of Frustrating Furtick. I call him *Future Furtick.*

Future Furtick is, in a word, perfection. If you could meet him, you'd want to marry him or vote for him for president. This guy is consistent and kind. He is disciplined but not rigid. He's fun loving but gets things done. He is people oriented and task driven in perfect harmony. He has an eight-pack, but he can enjoy a dessert on a social occasion. This guy is a specimen.

Future Furtick is the me I want to be. But he's also the me I know I'll never fully become.

So in my desperate effort to bridge the gap between Frustrating Furtick and Future Furtick, I've created yet another version of myself.

Fake Furtick.

Maybe I can't quite be Future Furtick, but I can fake it. I can pretend. I can pose. I can act like someone I'm not, because I think the real me is not good enough.

Fake Furtick doesn't even exist, but I've spent way too much time and energy trying to convince people that he does. Deep inside I suspect they see right through him, but I keep up the pretense anyway, because the real me is just too . . . frustrating.

So I keep faking it. I regurgitate the spiritual stuff that I have memorized even though it's not internalized. I smile and wave at the neighbors on the way out of the driveway even though I just yelled at my kids in the garage. I nod at stuff I don't understand instead of asking questions. I showcase strengths instead of acknowledging weakness. I'll do anything to keep up the image that I have my life together.

But I don't. At least not all the time. And certainly not in every area.

Yes, we should be positive people. Yes, we should be grateful, and we should celebrate victories, and we should have faith for the future. I'm not arguing against aspirations toward improvement.

Please hear me. I'm talking about a tendency to whitewash our weaknesses out of fear and insecurity. I'm talking about a deep, almost subconscious sense of failure and insufficiency that makes us pretend to be further along than we are. The kind of sideways energy that actually *impedes* us from pursuing the changes we should make.

But the pressure of perfection is pervasive. So we airbrush our images and Photoshop our failings. We art direct our personas, hoping to fool people into believing we are as perfect as they are.

But we aren't, and they aren't either, because no one is. We aren't photos, frozen in a fleeting moment of perfection for all to admire. We can't stage and light and crop and filter who we are.

Our lives are more like unedited movies. And our outtake reel is enormous, because we have no idea what we are doing much of the time. We are all feeling our way through life, one mistake and victory at a time.

We need to cut ourselves and one another some slack.

Because God is not in love with future you.

He's in love with the true you, even the most frustrating parts.

God can't bless Fake Furtick, the guy I pretend to be. And he certainly can't bless Future Furtick, the one who doesn't even exist and never will in all the ways I imagine.

But he can bless Frustrating Furtick, the beta version of me. He can love me and use me and transform me beyond my expectations. But for that to happen, I have to be real with myself.

And so do you.

No more pretending. No more posturing or posing. We must embrace who we are before we can become who we were meant to be.

Like Jacob, we can construct some pretty elaborate alternate identities. We dress in the finest clothes in Esau's closet. We learn how to talk the talk and walk the walk and wear the brands. But even if we get what we are after—the acceptance of our pretend selves—we just feel emptier than ever.

There are young ladies who Snapchat photos they never should have taken to keep the attention of boyfriends they never should have gone out with, only to find themselves betrayed and abandoned when the novelty wears off.

There are young men, good and sensitive guys, who play the parts of punks and thugs because they don't want people to think they aren't real men. But their artificially enhanced tough-guy personas only short-circuit the development of true compassion and courage.

There are wives who try to be Martha Stewart and Beyoncé simultaneously. They are extraordinary mothers and spouses, but they live under a constant cloud of failure because of the impossible image they measure themselves against.

There are husbands who work fourteen-hour days and max out credit cards and then end up with anxiety disorders because of their self-imposed stress to produce and provide.

That was never God's intent. That kind of pressure to pretend and perform doesn't come from the giver of every good and perfect gift.

We can learn how to build a facade. We can figure out how to cover up who we really are. Maybe we will fool other people. But we won't fool God. And we won't fool ourselves for long.

God is in love with the real you. That's why pretending is so pointless.

It is empowering to embrace who we really are, even when our third words look something like this:

I am terrified . . . I am lost . . . I am hurting . . . I am failing . . . I am insecure . . .

I am weak.

God's blessing is found in our honesty and transparency. He can't change or redeem our third words if we never admit to them.

God wants to bless the real you, with your weaknesses and problems and messes. The real you isn't perfect, but that's where the blessing is found. That's where God's grace is greatest and his strength is strongest.

EMBRACING JACOB

Jacob thought pretending to be Esau was the answer to his emptiness. Instead, his pretense created a web of new complications, including being exiled from his family and his home.

Jacob the pretender ended up spending the next twenty-one years living with his uncle Laban, who turned out to be a bigger trickster than Jacob ever thought about being. He made Jacob look downright gullible.

But eventually Jacob decided to return home and face his past. Along the way he had an encounter with God. And as a result he had an encounter with himself. Funny how that happens.

You can read the story in Genesis 32. After two decades of exile, Jacob was on his way home to attempt to make peace with Esau and see his parents again.

Not surprisingly, he was terrified. All the pretending and deceiving of his past still haunted him. The night before he was to meet with Esau, he was alone in the camp. He had sent his family separately for fear of what Esau might do.

Suddenly a stranger showed up and started wrestling with

him. That was odd. Even odder was the fact that the man turned out to be God. Many scholars believe it was actually Jesus in a preincarnate form.

They wrestled all night, and Jacob refused to let the man go. The man even dislocated Jacob's hip, but Jacob still wouldn't give up. It's unlikely Jacob knew exactly whom he was wrestling at this point. But he knew he had hold of something significant. More important, something significant had hold of him.

The man who had spent his whole life grabbing had been grabbed.

And in the heat of battle, Jacob declared, "I will not let you go unless you bless me" (verse 26).

Ninety-seven years of living hadn't weakened his resolve at all. The same tenacity he displayed in the womb was on display as he wrestled for his next blessing.

But this time he was holding on to the only One who truly has the power to bless.

Then, seemingly out of nowhere, the man asked, "What is your name?"

If I had been Jacob, I would be thinking, *This is a fine time to be asking. We've been fighting all night. You broke my hip. Now you want to get acquainted on a first-name basis?*

It seems a little random until you remember that Jacob had heard this question before. Twenty-one years earlier, when he went to Isaac to steal the blessing, Isaac had asked, "Who are you?"

On that occasion Jacob had replied, "I am Esau."

Years ago he was blessed by Isaac as Esau, but now it was time for Jacob to be blessed by God . . . as himself. The real blessing could only come by admitting who he really was.

"I am Jacob. Yes, that's me. That's my third word. I'm the deceiver. The backstabber. The heel grabber. The second born. The pretender. The broken. I am *Jacob.*"

This was the climactic conclusion of decades of deceit and pretending. Jacob finally recognized who he was, with all his imperfections and insufficiencies, and he held on to God for dear life.

And the Scriptures record the result.

When he finally embraced his name, God changed it! Or perhaps better said, God revealed his *true* identity. He showed him who he was meant to be all along.

"Your name will no longer be Jacob, but Israel" (verse 28). Israel means "triumphant with God." That's quite an upgrade from "heel grabber" and "deceiver."

Jacob was still Jacob. But in God, he was Israel.

Jacob still had weaknesses. But in God, he was strong.

It's the paradox of the third word. It's the dichotomy of destiny. When we embrace who we are, God works in, around, despite, and through our weaknesses to bless us.

It's funny to me that when Jacob asked the man for his name in exchange, the man refused to answer.

"Why do you ask my name?" the man replied (verse 29). And without answering the question Jacob deemed important, the man gave Jacob the blessing he sought.

"Then he blessed him there" (verse 29).

Then he blessed him.

When? When he owned his third word.

I am . . . Jacob.

Are you in a wrestling match right now with your own insecurities, fears, and failures? I believe that is the ideal meeting ground for God to show you who you really are and to remind you of who he really is. He will bless you there. In that place. When you say your real name.

Jacob had thought he was preparing to make peace with Esau. In reality, God brought him to the stream that night to make peace with himself. Jacob had planned to win the pardon of his brother by presenting him with elaborate gifts. But none of that turned out to be necessary.

When the two finally approached each other, the Bible says, "Esau ran to meet Jacob and embraced him; he threw his arms around his neck and kissed him. And they wept" (Genesis 33:4).

Standing face to face with the man he had spent his whole life struggling against, Jacob realized something I'm coming to understand more and more.

The only real battle I have to win . . . is the one within.

The battle is not with Esau. The battle is with me.

I believe that whatever external circumstances have brought you to this point in your journey, God desires to bless you, here and now. He desires to give you a new name and a new view of yourself as this new day dawns.

10

Just Call Me Jacob

A couple of years ago, Graham and Elijah asked me to tell them a Bible story just before bedtime. They were probably using this as a spiritual stall tactic, but I'm a sucker.

"Well there's this one story in the Bible about a wrestling match, but you probably wouldn't want to hear it," I teased.

"Yes sir, yes sir! Please tell us!"

So I began to tell them all about Jacob and Esau and how they wrestled in their mommy's belly.

And I went on to tell them all about the twins. I explained how Jacob was born trying to beat his brother and how he spent years of his life lying and deceiving to get what he wanted.

I told them about the time Jacob pretended to be Esau and tricked his dad into giving the blessing to him instead of Esau. During the story I happened to mention that Isaac would have put his right hand on Jacob's head when he blessed him, because it was the hand of authority, the hand of the firstborn.

The boys could definitely relate to all the competition and sibling rivalry. And when I got to the part about Jacob fighting the angel, they were totally into it. I may or may not have demonstrated a few gentle Ultimate Fighting Championship moves on them to make the scene come alive.

My story choice was a success. The boys were completely engrossed and bummed when it ended. But I didn't comprehend the extent to which they were paying attention until a few nights later. It was bedtime again, and I lay down with them for a minute so we could say our prayers.

Now don't be impressed, because I don't do this every time I pray for them, but that particular night I happened to put my hands on their heads while we were praying. I just happened to put my right hand on Elijah (the oldest) and my left on Graham (the youngest). I didn't mean anything by it.

But suddenly I felt Graham reach up and grab my right hand. He pulled it off Elijah's head and put it on his own.

Elijah figured out what was happening before I did. He yanked my hand back and said, "Oh no you don't!"

"Too late!" Graham gloated. Then came the line that made my night: "Just call me Jacob, sucker!"

I promise I'm not making this up. At the time he was five years old. Clearly our family needs prayer.

Just call me Jacob, sucker.

As my kids illustrated, thousands of years after the original Jacob-Esau wrestling match, nothing has changed. The same heel-grabbing, self-centered tendency is alive and well in all of us. No one has to teach us to fight for what we want. No one has to show us how to lie and deceive and steal.

It comes naturally.

Before Jacob and Esau were even born, they had their own UFC match going on in the womb. They started life grasping and grappling to get ahead. And they wrestled each other for most of their lives.

Why? Because we are innately self-focused. We are born thinking the solar system revolves around us and the universe exists to make us happy. Self-preservation and self-advancement are instinctive. Selfish motivation is our natural habitat.

That doesn't work well in the long run, by the way. Just look at Jacob. It took him most of his life to figure out that his maneuvering, manipulating, me-first mentality wasn't working.

Yet I find myself doing the same thing more often than I'd like. I obsess over my goals, my needs, my desires. I put up defenses and pretenses to protect my personal petty empire. I plan and plot to make sure I get my fair share out of life.

I know I'm not alone in this. It's the story of humanity.

Many people spend their whole lives conning and scheming and fighting. They carry the weight of their successes and failures every minute of every day. They do whatever it takes to get ahead, because if they don't look out for number one, who will?

That was Jacob. Always looking out for himself. Always the master of his fate. Always alone against the world.

But God didn't design us for that.

Beans, Birthrights, and Blessings

In the last chapter we looked at Jacob's propensity for pretense. He was an actor, a poser, a fake. Jacob had to learn to accept who he was before God could bless him. He became Israel when he learned to be Jacob.

Like his pretending, Jacob's tendency toward manipulation was a manifestation of his insecurities, of his reluctance to admit his weaknesses and trust in God's strength. Jacob thought he had to do everything on his own. He kept a death grip on his destiny because he didn't know any other way.

Jacob was always focused on one thing: getting what he wanted. Getting ahead. Being the first, richest, fastest, best.

That's why the name Jacob was so perfect for him. He was a heel grabber at heart. A deceiver by default.

We see this from the moment he and Esau were born, but it is especially evident in the story I referenced in the last chapter, when Esau traded his birthright to Jacob.

If you remember, Esau could hunt, but Jacob could cook. And one day that paid off for Jacob. Esau had been hunting. He came home famished and found Jacob cooking a pot of beans. So he asked Jacob for a bowl. Jacob, being the nice brother he was, happily agreed in exchange for one tiny thing.

His birthright.

Remember, in that culture the birthright was a double portion of the inheritance. Isaac was rich, so that was a lot of money. More than the biggest gourmet bowl of baked beans was worth.

The birthright rightfully belonged to the firstborn. But Jacob wanted it and would take it by any means necessary. He didn't care that he was stealing from his own brother or that he was earning a reputation for being a con man. He was looking out for number one.

Jacob saw an opening and took it. Unbelievably, Esau fell for it. That has to go down in history as one of the dumbest trades ever—right up there with the bum deal Portugal got in the Treaty of Tordesillas and the St. Louis Hawks' decision to send Bill Russell to the Celtics.

The decision says a lot about Esau, by the way. That's another topic for another time.

But the incident also says a lot about Jacob.

Deceiver was his name.

"Me first!" was his mantra.

Me First

Esau never forgot about Jacob's taking advantage of him in a moment of weakness. But Jacob didn't stop there. As we saw in the previous chapter, he still had his eye on the blessing. And as we saw, he ended up getting that as well.

That's the way this whole heel-grasping mentality works. When you are centered on yourself in life, when you have to be the best and the biggest to bolster a faulty self-worth, nothing is ever enough. You always have to have more. The damage this me-first, comparison-dominated attitude inflicts on relationships is insane. Jacob proved that time after time. In his quest for identity and value, he left a trail of broken, bleeding relationships behind him.

I've met men who are so insecure that they turn their wives and families into their personal empires. They always have to dominate. They always have to control. Everything is a competition, a challenge, a threat. They can't serve or love as they should because they spend all their energy defending their right to rule.

I've met parents who undermine their kids' futures because they can't get past their own feelings of inadequacy.

Do you see how damaging this is to relationships? We think that happiness comes from having more than someone else, but in our desperate pursuits to be king of the mountain, we can end up trampling the people we should have valued the most. We damage relationships in the name of advancement. Then we wonder why we feel so alone.

That's not living, in my opinion. That's surviving but at a terrible cost.

Whether we end up winners or losers, a me-against-the-world mentality is by definition a lonely way to live.

The fact that people around us have successes and advances doesn't mean we are failures. It doesn't take anything away from our value. And on the flip side, their failures don't make us more valuable.

In our effort to get ahead, we can end up losing sight of our own significance. We can forget that we are incalculably valuable in and of ourselves. We are important because God created us. Because he loves us. Because he chose us.

First Place, Last Place

After Jacob pretended to be Esau and stole his father's blessing, he ended up living with his uncle Laban for twenty-one years. As I mentioned earlier, Laban was the king of cons.

Here is just one example. Jacob fell in love with Laban's daughter Rachel. He agreed to work for Laban for seven years in exchange for her hand in marriage. But on their wedding night, Laban pranked Jacob. Only there was nothing funny about it.

Laban gave Jacob his older daughter, Leah, instead of Rachel. Apparently Jacob was too drunk to notice. When Jacob woke up in the morning next to Leah, he was understandably furious. So Laban told Jacob he'd give him Rachel too—for another seven years of work.

The cosmic touché. Jacob had met his match.

That was just the beginning of the drama between them. It was a sorry story of lies, manipulation, and deceit that stretched over decades. And at the end of twenty-one years of this, Jacob found himself fleeing in fear.

Again.

Have you ever noticed how complicated life gets when everyone is manipulating everyone else? When everyone is trying to use everyone else to get what they think they want?

It's complicated. It's confusing. And it's exhausting.

Jesus once said something pretty powerful about the way things work in his kingdom: "Many who are first will be last, and many who are last will be first" (Matthew 19:30).

In other words, it's not always the ones who get ahead who are ahead.

We read that and we say, "Come on, Jesus, that's not how the world works. Haven't you seen *Talladega Nights*? Didn't you hear what Ricky Bobby's dad said to him when he was peeling out?"

"If you ain't first, you're last."

And Jesus might respond, "Decent movie but wrong philosophy."

In God's kingdom trying to be first is the best way to be last. But learning to serve, to wait, to be humble and secure in God is the path to true success.

Living a me-first life is miserable. I speak from personal experience, and I've had plenty. If everything is about you, and your ego is so big that it takes all your time to protect it and polish it, and you need everybody around you to prop up your self-esteem, you're headed for misery.

Heel grabbing is a horrible business. It's miserable to be trapped inside self-centered illusions. It's miserable never to have a bigger thought than "What's best for me?" It's miserable to be disconnected from the people around you because all you can think about is your own convenience.

And it's not just that the me-first approach is wrong. The problem is, in the end it doesn't even work.

Jesus said on another occasion, "What good is it for someone to gain the whole world, and yet lose or forfeit their very self?" (Luke 9:25).

In other words, "What good is it, Jacob, if you grasp after stuff, status, success, and security only to find yourself more lost than ever? What good is it, if in the process of grabbing and groping and grasping, you lose yourself?"

Axl Rose might not be a saint, but he was right about this: "Just because you're winnin' don't mean you're the lucky ones."[10]

I had an experience several years ago that helped redefine the way I see true success. I was invited to be part of a ministry event featuring several very well-known pastors. These guys were some of the most famous in the church world today. At a dinner before the event, I found myself wondering why I was included, because I felt a little outclassed. And I was the youngest one in the room by more than a decade.

The conversation was lively, and everyone seemed to be enjoying it. Then suddenly the discussion took a turn I wasn't prepared for.

When the host asked, "How would you describe your overall feelings about ministry at this point?" the mood of the room grew a little gray.

As each preacher weighed in, I was shocked and a little saddened that the majority responded with some version of this conclusion: being in ministry is like being in prison.

It wasn't until a few days after the event that I realized the impact the exchange had on me. These are good men at the top of their field. They help people, have purpose, and are making a tremendous difference. It's not that they are hypocrites. It just goes to show that all the success in the world, even when you're doing God's work, doesn't guarantee a satisfied soul. These men, whose spiritual maturity many envy, were silently miserable.

My point isn't that they are all manipulators and now God is punishing them for building their ministries on the wrong foundation. Nor am I saying that doing what God calls us to do will always feel like fun. That would be a pretty hard case to make in light of the life of the apostle Paul or Jesus himself.

I share the story only because that exchange brought me to an important determination. I decided if that's what it takes to build a big ministry, I don't want it. I refuse to give my life to helping others live in freedom and secretly feel as if I'm locked in solitary confinement.

Jesus's words resonated in my heart and mind that night:

What good is it?

If you get what you want and then don't want what you've got, what's the point? There has to be a better way.

Yet many of us never stop to consider our course. So we lose ourselves—the real us, the authentic us, the valuable us—because we are so desperate to claw our way to the top.

But what good is it, Jesus asks us, if we lose who we are just to gain money, popularity, church attendance, Instagram followers, or anything else?

God didn't design life to work this way. And he didn't design us to carry the entire weight of our destinies on our own.

That's his job. And he's way better at it than we are.

That might be why some of us feel so burned out and stressed out all the time. Maybe we've been using people we are supposed to love. Maybe we've been trying to control our world when we should relax a little and let God be God.

Maybe our prison cells are locked from the inside.

The Player Gets Played

When Jacob first arrived at Laban's house, he had nothing. When he left, he was a wealthy man. He had family, flocks, and possessions.

That didn't happen just because he was so clever. It happened because God had decided to bless him.

If you read the story, you'll see that both Laban and Jacob recognized that Jacob's blessings came from God's hand. Uncle and nephew spent years circling each other, stalking each other, maneuvering and manipulating and trying to outwit one another. But in the end it wasn't Laban or Jacob who got the last laugh. It was God. He outplayed them both.

God has a way of doing what he wants. Have you noticed? We have our strategies and plans. We think four steps ahead, and we move our pawns and our bishops and our knights, and we impress ourselves with our aptitude.

And then God says, "Checkmate."

The me-first mentality says that to get ahead in life, we have to be first. We have to be cunning and even cutthroat. Jacob learned the hard way that sooner or later the trickster gets tricked and the player gets played.

Some people have been pretending and defending and deceiving for so long they can't imagine letting God take control. They've built their lives around the philosophy that the spoils go to the strongest, to the smartest, to the most manipulative.

Maybe you feel that way. I know I have at times.

Maybe you wish that you could let your guard down. That you could just enjoy each day instead of always fighting and striving for first place.

But, you might think, if you don't watch out for yourself, who will?

Take a close look at your third words. Do they look something like this?

I am strong.

I am independent.

I am alone.

I am self-made.

Not to be critical, but those simply aren't true. They might feel true, and I am by no means minimizing your contribution to your success. But ultimately are you really the reason for your success?

Or is it God?

God's blessing on our lives has far more to do with who he is than who we are. That was the whole point of his *I AM* revelation to Moses.

A manipulative outlook on life is a result of not understanding the true source of our blessings. Our blessings come from God, and they rest on our real selves.

This gives us permission to lower our defenses. Remember the passage from 2 Corinthians that we looked at several chapters ago?

When I am weak, then I am strong.

In the context Paul was pleading for God to set him free from his weakness. But God said no.

Then God went on to explain his reasoning. In God, Paul's weakness was no longer weakness. It was strength. It was the very place God would accomplish the most.

I'm convinced that God lets some of our weaknesses hang around because they offer us a window into our need for him. They remind us to turn to God constantly instead of trusting solely in ourselves.

None of us controls our fate. We influence it greatly, but we don't control it.

Think about it. We don't determine the place of our birth. We don't single-handedly run the economy or governments in those places. We can't stop natural disasters. We can't predict the decisions of people around us. We can't guarantee our good health. We don't know the day we will die.

But God does all those things and more.

We can't go more than a few hours without rest and sleep, but the universe doesn't fall apart while we are curled up under the covers. God is still there, guiding, protecting, and watching over our tiny, finite selves. He must get a good laugh out of the size of our egos sometimes.

The psalmist recognized God's infinite control when he wrote:

> I lift up my eyes to the mountains—
>   where does my help come from?
> My help comes from the LORD,
>   the Maker of heaven and earth.
>
> He will not let your foot slip—
>   he who watches over you will not slumber;
> indeed, he who watches over Israel
>   will neither slumber nor sleep.
>
> The LORD watches over you—
>   the LORD is your shade at your right hand;

the sun will not harm you by day,
nor the moon by night.

The LORD will keep you from all harm—
he will watch over your life;
the LORD will watch over your coming and going
both now and forevermore. (Psalm 121:1–8)

Our sense of identity and value must take God into account. If we don't, we usually end up vacillating between delusions of grandeur and the depths of despair. One minute we are superheroes; the next minute we are waving a white flag.

Consider this: we are never so awesome that success is inevitable, and we are never so terrible that success is impossible.

In both our strengths and weaknesses, God makes the difference. Our successes come from his blessings. We can't take all the credit. We aren't smart enough or strong enough to achieve all of that on our own.

At the same time, our weaknesses are not insurmountable for him. There is hope even in our failures and frailties, because God's third words trump ours every time.

GRABBING GOD

Involving God in our identities and our endeavors is the heart of being qualified. Of measuring up. Of being valuable and approved and significant.

This truth is woven through Jacob's life. Remember his showdown with the angel? The blessing came when Jacob owned up to his own identity, both the good and the bad.

Sometimes we think we have to be perfect to convince God to bless us. So we strive for holiness, which is right, but we do it in order to convince God to bless us, which is wrong.

In case you are wondering, we don't have to convince God to bless us. He *loves* to bless us. And we certainly can't be good enough to deserve all the things he gives us.

According to that mentality, Jacob would have been the last man on earth God would have blessed. But God blessed the *real* Jacob. He blessed Frustrating Jacob. Not Fake Jacob or Future Jacob or Perfect Jacob. God took care of him despite his weaknesses, despite his pretenses, and despite his sinfulness.

God blessed Jacob because of who God is and how much God loved him, not because Jacob was so clever or hardworking. I'm convinced God would have blessed Jacob just as much if he had trusted God from the very beginning. And the blessing would have come with a lot less anguish and angst. Jacob spent his life like a cat burglar trying to pry open the windows of blessing with a crowbar, and meanwhile God was inviting him to walk in the front door as an honored guest.

Here's what I find fascinating about Jacob's encounter with the angel. Jacob had always been the heel grabber. Jacob had always been the one who chased and grasped at others. Now God was grabbing hold of him.

I think that is a key to this whole story, actually. You can spend your life clutching and clawing and fighting, but what you really need is for God to grab you. For grace to grasp you.

Jacob was born grasping at heels, and that was how he had lived his life. But now God was holding on to him, and he was holding on to God, the only one who really had the power to bless him. He should have done that much earlier.

It's funny. The same heel-grabbing tenacity that had made him a schemer and a con man was now working for him, because he had it channeled in the right direction. Isn't that how God works though? He takes the very characteristics we tend to look down on, and he uses them for our good.

Maybe, just maybe, it's time for you to let go of some things and just hold on to God.

Let go of what people think.

Let go of your past.

Let go of pretenses.

Let go of schemes and manipulation.

And while you're at it, let go of one more thing. It's one of the most insidious traps of all, as you're about to see. It's called comparison.

11

The Problem with Pinterest

I have a problem with Pinterest.

For those who might not be familiar with Pinterest, it's a website where you can create and share collections of images or links that interest you. It's a popular place to find ideas for everything from trips to DIY projects to recipes, because you can look at the cool things other people have done and then try to imitate them.

PC Magazine defines Pinterest this way: "A socially oriented photo-sharing site in the form of an online pinboard."[11]

Here's an alternate definition. I may or may not have written it myself. "Pinterest is a visually driven social media platform strategically designed for nonstop, twenty-four-hours-a-day, seven-days-a-week reminders that your kids are not as well dressed as your neighbors' kids, that your home is decorated in the most amateur fashion imaginable, that the pictures you take are bland and artless, that you did a terrible job planning your wedding, and that you live a generally tedious, monotonous existence—unlike everyone else, whose lives are categorically awesome at all times."

Yes, I have a bit of a problem with Pinterest.

Don't get me wrong. I am not against social media in general or even Pinterest in particular. Social media is just a tool. And the results it generates reflect the intention of the user. And that can be a problem.

Why? Because as humans we tend to compare ourselves to other people way too much, and social media isn't helping.

The problem I have with Pinterest is that it's a place where people present their perfection for all of us to observe. It's the mind-set that Pinterest helps to create. But often it's an incomplete picture of the real story. So we compare our underwhelming reality to their staged, cropped, filtered photos, and we end up feeling terrible about ourselves. Or we upload our own manufactured reality in an effort to project a perfection we are far from achieving.

I recently found out about a site called Pinterest Fail. I like it a lot better than the real Pinterest, actually. It shows real-life attempts by mere mortals to re-create what they found on Pinterest. The results range from hilarious to terrifying. But at least it leaves us with a feeling that there's hope for the rest of us.

Maybe you don't use Pinterest. But do you do the same thing with HGTV? With *People* magazine? With Instagram or Facebook? Do you look at your neighbor or your pastor or the superfit, supercute team mom and wonder why you can't seem to measure up to their abilities, achievements, and understated swagger?

Obviously the problem of comparison isn't limited to one particular medium. It's a mind-set. The only problem with Pinterest is the problem within us. It's the perfect platform for our tendency to pretend, to pose, and to perform, all in an effort to bolster a shaky self-esteem.

It has to stop, and Jacob's life teaches us why. To recap, we've been looking at how the story of Jacob illustrates some not-so-healthy human tendencies, specifically, *pretending* and *manipulating.* The other amigo in this little trio is *comparing.*

All three of these are negative results of basing our self-worth on the wrong things. Of not knowing or accepting who we really are, including our imperfections. Of not letting God's grace be our qualifier.

Jacob was pretty much doomed to be a victim of comparison from the moment he was born. It was almost inevitable just because he was a twin. Throughout his life he and Esau were compared and contrasted, loved or rejected, based not on their own merits but on how they measured up to each other.

I have a friend who is a twin, and she tells me that comparison was the story of her life growing up. She and her sister hardly had their own identities because to everyone around them they were simply "the twins." People invariably commented on who was skinnier, faster, smarter, friendlier, taller. They shared a room, shared friends, and had shared a womb. Comparison and competition weren't just tendencies; they were a way of life.

Jacob, Esau, and the twins of the world aren't the only ones with that lifestyle, though. We are all affected by it. Our culture runs on comparisons and contrasts. We love standings and rankings. And just when we think we're about to hit the target, the target moves.

All About That -Er

Jacob defined success by how he measured up to others. If he had less than his brother, he was a failure. If he had more, he was a success.

The philosopher C. S. Lewis addressed this issue when he said that we don't actually take pride in the possession itself but in having more of it than someone else.[12] It's not enough just to be thin. We have to be thinner than she is. It's not enough to be ripped. We have to be more ripped than he is. We have to be richer, smarter, more popular, more accomplished.

That's a problem.

Anytime our third words are comparisons, anytime they start with the word *more* or end with the suffix *-er,* alarms, sirens, and flashing red lights should go off inside our heads.

I am wealthier.

I am faster.

I am more beautiful.

I am more influential.

I am more spiritual.

Those aren't the kind of third words we need. Since when did being bigger, better, and badder come to mean success?

Using comparisons to define our value is intrinsically insecure. It's a dead giveaway that our value systems are wrong.

We do this more often than we realize. Our third words frequently hinge on other people. We evaluate and rate ourselves based on other people in our world.

Sometimes we compare ourselves to people who are worse just

to prove how amazing we are. Other times we compare ourselves to people who are better just to feed our internal pity party. Neither extreme is logical or accurate, and both are corrosive to our souls.

The first one produces complacency. If I look at someone else and realize I'm better at something than that person is, I tend to think I've arrived in that area. That I can stop growing and stop working. But maybe God has called me to do more. Maybe he has given me a greater capacity.

The second one produces condemnation. If I look at the accomplishments, spirituality, or talents of others and see that I fall short, I can end up discouraged and insecure about who I am. I can feel unqualified even though God is perfectly happy with where I am.

It is also one of the most relative and subjective activities I can think of. Think you are really good at something? That's great, but consider this: there are seven billion people on the planet, and the odds are, a few *million* people are better than you at your particular area of expertise.

I have a friend who loves to go sailing with his wife each summer for three weeks. To me that sounds like hell. Not the wife part—geez, people. I'm talking about three weeks on a boat. To each his own, but that's not my thing.

However, my friend loves it. And he said an interesting thing happens when he takes his boat out. "You know, I start out each time thinking how blessed I am to have three weeks off from work, a wife I want to spend three weeks with, and a charming little boat. But without fail, within the first few days, I'll come across somebody with a boat that's so nice even their *lifeboat* puts our whole boat to shame. And they're not taking three weeks off work, because they never have to work another day in their lives."

The last line he said stuck with me. "The thing is, there's always someone with a better boat."

Now, you may be thinking #richpeopleproblems about the whole scenario I just described. But it's just a metaphor to illustrate that no matter how much "-er" you get, there's always someone who is "-er-er."

And on the flip side, no matter how bad you are at something, millions are worse off than you. There is somebody who would give anything to be in your situation with your strengths. As I told our church one time, somebody out there is praying to have your problems.

Comparison is a silent killer. It steals our joy and undermines our relationships. It causes us to criticize events we should celebrate, reject people we should learn from, and resent ideas we should embrace.

God's qualification of us doesn't depend on other people. He doesn't leverage the failure of others to make us feel better about ourselves. He doesn't tie our success or approval to the performance of those around us.

God's third words flow from his divine vision for our lives. He knows who we are and what we are capable of, and he values us just as we are. He knows how many talents he's given us to multiply and invest back into the world around us.

It's worth noting that the culture of comparison is not unique to the Pinterest age. It's been around for thousands of years. It's a natural result of human insecurity and pride.

Paul had to address this attitude in the church at Corinth. False teachers had come into the church and were undermining Paul. They were trying to convince the Corinthians that they were more qualified than Paul and that the church should listen to their teachings rather than his. The crazy part is they based their argument not on the truth of their message but on their own qualifications as compared to Paul's.

That didn't sit well with Paul. Not because he needed to justify himself or defend himself, but because his beloved friends were being led into error and spiritual captivity. They were falling prey to a spirit of comparison.

So Paul wrote to the church: "We do not dare to classify or compare ourselves with some who commend themselves. When they measure themselves by themselves and compare themselves with themselves, they are not wise" (2 Corinthians 10:12).

And by "not wise" he meant "really stupid." This truth applies to all areas of our lives, not just our doctrine. Comparing ourselves and measuring ourselves against ourselves is pointless. It proves nothing. It accomplishes nothing.

How do you define success? How do you know when you are qualified? Do you take pride and pleasure in simply being you? In becoming the person God made you to be? Or are you constantly comparing yourself to someone in your life or maybe to *everyone* in your life?

How do you respond when people around you find success?

Do you congratulate them and celebrate them with a sincere heart? Or do you secretly suspect their accomplishments are proof of your inadequacy?

The sister of a friend recently came to visit her. The sister pointed to one of the Christmas cards on the fridge and asked, "Who is that?"

"Oh, that's my friend Amy," my friend replied.

"Oh no," the sister said, "I wouldn't want a friend that pretty."

That was a couple of years ago, and the sister will still ask my friend, "So, how's Pretty Amy doing?" Even though she's never met her.

Other than the obvious lesson that we don't have to say everything we think, this way of thinking shows a lot about the way we're wired.

God wants you to discover the freedom of simply being yourself. Of living beyond comparisons. Of finding your identity and security not in how you stack up against those around you but in your relationship with him.

You Can't Hide from Oprah

Comparison inevitably leads to competition. Jacob and Esau couldn't be clearer illustrations of this. They spent their lives competing against each other: for blessings, for the birthright, for parental approval. Their sibling rivalry reached homicidal levels. And even after decades of separation, the suspicion and deception never disappeared.

I mentioned earlier that when Jacob wrestled the angel, he

was on his way home. And he was terrified. He knew he was going to face his old sins against Esau, and he thought Esau would try to kill him and his family.

Behind Jacob was Laban, and in front of him was Esau. Two relationships destroyed by manipulation and competition.

Jacob was caught in the middle. It was a mess of his own making. Sure, he had accumulated massive wealth. He had wives and children. He had status. He was bigger and better than anyone in his life.

But the night the angel found him, he was scared, alone, and vulnerable.

That's what a life of competition invariably produces.

Competition is not wrong in and of itself, of course. And in most areas of life, a certain degree of competition can be healthy. Even exciting. After all, the same Paul who said not to compare also talked about the virtues of running to win the prize. But the competition must be focused on the right things, and it must be under control. You can't lose yourself in the midst of the competition.

One of the most famous competitors in recent history is Lance Armstrong. He is a cycling legend, having won the Tour de France a record seven consecutive times. Accusations of using performance-enhancing drugs followed him throughout his career, but he consistently denied them, and repeated investigations failed to prove anything. Eventually his drug use was exposed, though, and he was stripped of his titles.

The first time he confessed to doping was in an Oprah interview, which goes to show that you can hide from the government and you can hide from the media, but you can't hide from Oprah.[13] She'll bring you to justice, son.

I'm not here to criticize Lance Armstrong. I don't have any rocks to throw at anyone. None of us would want people following us around and tracking our contradictions. And I haven't been on a bike since I was fourteen (except one time in Brooklyn when my friend Carl almost got me killed), so I'm not an expert on any aspects of cycling. But what got me about that interview was the idea of a supreme competitor who was stripped of everything he had competed for.

Oprah asked Armstrong if he thought it was possible to have won seven Tours de France without doping.

He responded, "Not in that generation. . . . I didn't invent the culture, but I didn't try to stop the culture, and that's my mistake, and that's what I have to be sorry for."

He went on to say, "My ruthless desire to win at all costs served me well on the bike, but the level it went to, for whatever reason, is a flaw. That desire, that attitude, that arrogance."[14]

They talked about the culture of doping. To Armstrong, doping was as necessary in order to compete as putting air in his tires or water in his water bottle. Everybody did it, so he was just leveling the playing field.

Oprah asked him about the thirteen years of lies and coverups, and he told her that the lie just kept gaining momentum, and he had to repeat it. The pressure to maintain the perfect image before his fans and the media was too great. He admitted, "I lost myself in all of that."[15]

I lost myself. That's the phrase. I don't want to lose myself in my pursuit of success and victory. I don't want to sacrifice what is really important in an effort to gain status.

Competition and comparison might seem harmless and even fun for a while. But they have a way of catching up and biting us on the backside. When we define ourselves based on how far ahead of the pack we are, we instantly set ourselves up for failure. Sooner or later we encounter someone better than we are. A bigger boat. A prettier Amy. That sends our self-image plummeting, and we either slink away in defeat or snarl and bite until we regain our status.

Please hear me. We will never be "enough better" than everyone else to be secure.

Ever.

We will always have to fight off contenders for first place. We will view everyone around us as competitors. And we'll do anything it takes to maintain our lead. We'll miss a million blessings in the meantime.

Lance Armstrong felt he had no choice but to cheat because of the culture of competition around him. And as a result, he ended up sacrificing the very things he worked for. He lost his victories, his reputation, and his control. He lost himself.

How about us? Are we driven by a culture of competition that obligates us to lose ourselves in order to win? Is the pressure to perform and produce really so irresistible? Or is it possible to find our fulfillment in Jesus? To have a holy confidence that is not borrowed from the opinion of others?

Full of It

The answer to the incessant voices of comparison and competition is to know God as our qualifier and our approver.

As my counselor used to tell me, it's checking in, even a thousand times a day if that's what it takes, and asking God, "Are we good?"

And then breathing in the affirmation, "We're good."

And agreeing with his assessment: *Then I'm good.*

Paul said this to the Colossians: "In Christ all the fullness of the Deity lives in bodily form, and in Christ you have been brought to fullness" (2:9–10).

As Christians, we might not have too much trouble believing verse 9. We know Jesus was the expressed revelation and the manifest image of God, so much so that he could say to his disciples, "Anyone who has seen me has seen the Father" (John 14:9). Everything that resided in God from the time he spoke the world into existence was demonstrated in the person of Jesus. Jesus was without sin; he was complete righteousness.

We often have trouble believing verse 10, though: that *we* have been brought to fullness in Christ. But verse 9 about Jesus cannot be true unless verse 10 about us is true as well. They're right there in the same Bible.

In essence, Paul says, "Let me tell you how full and complete Jesus is." Then, in the same breath, he says, "And let me tell you how full and complete you are."

He doesn't pause. He doesn't qualify his statement. In the

context of the brilliance of Christ, he makes a declaration of fullness over you and me.

That's the antidote to the absurdity of this Snapchat society in which we have to make our lives look interesting for ten seconds so everyone will think we're having fun.

God wants to speak a different reality over our lives. He wants us to know and believe that the fullness of Christ has been given to us. It is finished. It is accomplished. And nothing can change that.

This is the deathblow to the spirit of competition that rules our lives apart from Christ. If I have fullness in Christ, if I have everything God has in Christ, if I'm full of love and joy and affirmation and blessing and strength and Jesus, then there is no need for comparison and no place for competition.

If I'm full of Jesus and Jesus is full of God, what do I have to prove to anyone? What do you have to prove?

Nothing.

That's the freedom we have in Christ. That's the security we have when God is our qualifier. That is also how we are simultaneously both unqualified and qualified. We are unqualified in the eyes of the world but declared more than qualified through Christ.

I have a little series of questions I take myself through when I feel the spirit of competition rising inside me. It's not just in the big areas of life, either. Sometimes it happens during a random conversation. I'll feel the need to tell a story that is bigger and better than someone else's story. I'll find myself trying to showcase my importance and significance rather than affirming and celebrating someone else's. I'll find myself inwardly happy about someone else's struggle because it makes me feel better about my own. And I'll realize that once again I'm falling into the trap of comparison.

Here are some questions I ask myself to break that orbit:

1. What am I trying to prove?
2. To whom?
3. For what?

These questions stop me in my tracks. They break the spirit of competition in my life.

For example, what am I trying to establish when I tell somebody how big my church is? What am I trying to prove? My value? My calling? My significance? My qualifications?

"You have a big church. Congratulations. Cool."

Usually about thirty seconds after I say something like that, a cloud of self-disgust comes over me because I realize how carnal and shallow my motives were. What good did that just do? What did either of us gain from that conversation? And why did I feel so compelled to shoehorn the size of my ministry into the conversation?

True freedom in Christ comes when you realize you have nothing to prove to anyone, because in Christ, God fully approves of you.

And by the way, you don't learn this just once in life. That's why I've been repeating it throughout this book. Life has a way of laying siege to your security, to your confidence in Christ. The only prevention I have found for the corruption of constant comparison that eats away at your soul is returning to the simple truth that God alone is our qualifier.

The temptation to prove yourself doesn't go away as you climb the ladder of success. It gets magnified, and the prospects of falling get scarier. There will always be pressure to conform, to perform, to measure up.

But God can fill us with a fullness that can't be stripped away. Without it, we'll always feel empty, no matter how much we produce or consume. We might get seven trophies, but we'll still be peddling toward a shallow superiority. We will lose ourselves in our search for the fullness that Jesus has already given us.

What are you trying to prove? To whom? And why?

Trying to prove anything to anyone is a waste of time. That's a bold statement, but it's true. If the people you are out to impress already love you, then it's a waste of time because you are already valued and accepted by them. And if they don't love you, then it's a waste of time, because even if you win their approval, what have you gained? If their love is something you had to earn, they don't really love you.

As a pastor and preacher, I have a public role. And I'm going to be very transparent here: one of the challenges I face consistently is not worrying about whether people like me. I go through this all the time, because while I'm up there trying to help people hear from God, sometimes a little voice in my head starts saying, *I wonder what they think of me. Do they think I'm smart? Funny? Anointed? Gifted? Deep?*

It's distracting, it's diabolical, and it's destructive. The truth is, I don't want people to see me. I want them to see Jesus. But I can get in my own way.

I often worry and wonder and work as if the opinion of people is the ultimate source of my qualifications. It's utter madness. Why would I try to get a medal from somebody who is not authorized to give a medal? Medals like that will get stripped away at the podium of eternity. So what good are they?

You might not speak in front of live audiences, but I bet you've felt the same pressure to please. The same pressure to live up to other people's arbitrary and often unexpressed expectations and standards.

Recently God gave me a thought that was so liberating. As I was preparing to minister to a group of people, worrying about how I would come across and if I would live up to their ideals, it was as if the Lord said to me:

I didn't bring you here to meet their expectations.

I brought you here to be my expression.

My only goal is to be a faithful reflection of his image in me. That's all I can do. And that's enough.

Because even if we prove ourselves to people, what exactly have we gained? If they decide they like us, it's going to take just as much work to keep their good favor as it did to win it. Maybe more. So what did we win?

Imagine their thought process. *Congratulations. Now you can keep impressing me so I can continue to think you're a pretty good person. Unless of course I change my standards, which I will do without warning. Then you'll have to start over.*

Something has to change. We can't spend our lives hoping people like us. We have to find our fullness in Christ. If we are full of Christ and someone doesn't like us, guess what? It's their loss. They are missing out on what God has put in us.

I'm not talking about being cocky. I'm talking about being complete in Christ. About being confident in his calling. About being content with the gifts and abilities we have rather than comparing ourselves to someone else.

When you know you're called, you no longer play for the applause of anyone or anything. Your only desire is the affirmation of a heavenly Father who loves you when you're broke, who loves you in your sexual dysfunction, who loves you even when you have an issue you can't seem to get past.

When you have that affirmation from someone who knows you completely and loves you anyway, the world doesn't have a medal big enough or shiny enough to tempt you. The spirit of comparison and competition is broken, because you know you have a higher calling.

So what are we trying to prove?

We're already approved. We're already qualified.

Just the Beginning

True freedom in Christ comes when we realize that without him we are spiritually bankrupt, but in him we have all things. We declare that truth every day in every situation. We believe it no matter what our emotions or circumstances try to tell us or how good or bad we feel or what successes or failures we happen to be experiencing at the moment. God's completeness is what matters the most.

We can never fill our emptiness from a place of emptiness. Only Jesus can fill us. Only Christ can qualify us. And when he does, nothing can take that away.

When we start from a place of completeness in Christ, everything changes. God's approval and calling qualify us to live a new kind of life.

First, we are free to truly love. Not the empty, transient love the world offers. Not a love based on performance and qualification. Rather, the unconditional love that God has given us, the love that he calls us to share with others.

We are also free to truly serve the Lord. Not because we are afraid that God will reject us, but because we are overflowing with thanksgiving for all he's done for us. It's our unforced and organic response to God's goodness.

And finally we are free to truly succeed. God is happy for our successes and our strengths, but he's even happier that he is our treasure, our friend, and our source of fulfillment. The best way to be successful and affirmed and fulfilled is to be so full of God that we don't need the success.

In Jesus we are fully forgiven. We are free from all shame and condemnation. We are fully loved and accepted by God. We are secure in God's calling.

In comparison to that, our weaknesses and insecurities disappear. God is for us, so nothing and no one can prevail over us. We don't need to spend one more day trying to prove ourselves, because we already have God's approval through Jesus's gift of righteousness.

Are you ready to embrace who you are in order to become who God has called you to be? Are you willing to cease striving for approval and instead trust in God, your qualifier?

If so, this is only the beginning.

Reaching the Goal

A couple of times a year I teach a class called Generation for a small group of students in our church. During one of the sessions, I ask the students to teach me how to sound cool.

I've given up hopes of actually *being* cool, of course. I'm in my thirties, which is essentially prehistoric to my students. But it's a good way to connect and get conversations started. And if they can help me sound cool, at least in spurts, it's a win-win, right?

So I'll say, "Hey, I need a vocabulary update. My children aren't teenagers yet, so what do kids these days say?"

I never thought I'd use the phrase "Kids these days." It's kind of depressing.

One of my recent Generation groups was very helpful. They taught me the correct usage of *Bae,* for example. They also taught me the meaning of the term *on fleek.*

I said, "Use that one in a sentence. I don't get it."

Someone replied, "Okay, your sneakers are on fleek."

"Oh, it's like *on point.*"

"Huh?"

I thought, *Wow, I'm old.*

Then one of them spoke up and said, "Goals."

I said, "Goals? You think that's a new word? Come on, man, I'm not that old . . ."

He said, "No, no. The hashtag. People use it for everything now. You can put it on almost anything. You know, hashtag *goals*."

I was intrigued. So I searched the hashtag on Instagram. The student was right. It was everywhere.

Then I decided to do some more official research on the hashtag, an act that is inherently uncool, but you have to start somewhere. I even came across an article in *Elle* magazine about the trend. (I'd already turned in my cool card, so why not my man card too?) The writer, Justine Harman, shared a great insight and explanation:

> The trending term [#goals], which also pairs neatly with prefixes such as "life," "body," "hair," "squad," and "relationship," is tongue-in-cheek, lazy, and purposefully self-deprecating. A "goal" in this context is something aspirational and outlandish, a perceived quality of life that we categorize as unattainable.[16]

Here's an example of what she's describing. Let's say you see a picture of Jay-Z and Beyoncé in their Gulfstream 650 cuddling under a blanket made of organic zebra skin, and you comment on the photo using the hashtag "goals."

It's a way of saying: *yeah right* and *I wish* all at once.

And it left me wondering, *Isn't this a dangerous perversion of the real purpose of a goal?*

I know it's meant to be playful, and this certainly isn't a rant about "kids these days." But it got me thinking. The *goals* meme is a tragic commentary on how the human race handles goals we don't feel qualified to achieve. It describes how a lot of us react mentally and emotionally when we compare where we are now to where we wish we could be. Our unfulfilled goals become the voices that mock us. They are a commentary on our failure and a reminder that we aren't good enough—and never will be.

Isn't the proliferation of ridiculous #goals just a modern manifestation of Jacob's struggle? He didn't know how to handle the gap between who he was and who he wanted to be. From the womb he had goals that were literally beyond his grasp. He knew he was called to greatness, to wealth, to influence. But he was the second born. He was the runt. He was the underestimated overachiever.

So as we have seen, he spent decades pretending, manipulating, and comparing in an effort to gain by self-effort what God could have given him by grace.

But then he wrestled an angel.

And he accepted himself.

And he got a new name.

I wish I could tell you that was a definitive, once-and-for-all transformation in Jacob. That by embracing his identity he was forever freed from his struggles and his humanity. That Jacob became Israel and lived happily ever after.

But I can't, because it doesn't work that way, despite what the Grimm brothers tell us. Fairy tales say that stories end neatly and loose ends get tied up. That dragons are killed, villains are banished, and heroes and heroines get married and rule pastel-colored kingdoms.

But in real life the line between villain and hero is a bit blurred. Just like with Jacob.

In real life, heroes have defining moments of self-realization and then turn around and do the same destructive thing again. Just as Jacob did.

And in real life, the story doesn't really end. Because in real life, the goal isn't to live happily ever after. It isn't to finish the plot, resolve the conflict, and then roll the credits. There is more to life than eliminating weaknesses or coming out on top.

It's miserable to live in a confusing limbo between reality and destiny, hoping and praying and working toward a happily ever after that we will never reach until we understand what the goal really is.

Obviously, having goals is not the problem. Goals are helpful tools to motivate our actions and to measure our progress. As humans we are goal-oriented creatures, and I believe God created us that way precisely because he is a God of goals.

Many of us are actually really good at setting goals and even at reaching those goals. That's not the issue.

The issue is that, like Jacob, we don't always have the *right* goals to start with.

We can reach all the goals we want, but if they are the wrong goals, we still end up in the wrong place. A commitment to the wrong goals may create an illusion of progress, but it won't bring the reward of true fulfillment.

It's one thing to ask, "Am I reaching my goal?" But it's another to ask, "Is it a good goal? Is it the best goal?"

In a goal-obsessed society it's important to be intentional about asking those questions. Where are our goals taking us? Is what we're making life all about really what life should be all about? Are our goals worth obtaining? Are the people we're envious of even happy?

Maybe it's time to stop the rat race. Get off the hamster wheel. Quit following the lemmings.

(I just realized that all those metaphors revolve around rodents. I should improve my literary skills. #goals)

I was talking to a mom whose kids have all left home. She told me what every empty nester tells Holly and me: "Treasure every moment. Time flies by."

That's easy for you to say, I always think. *Yours are gone. Mine are still wrecking stuff.*

This woman continued, "I look back at my parenting, and I see that I often had the wrong goals."

I said, "For example?"

She said, "For example, why did I think the biggest goal of day-to-day life was to have a clean carpet? For the twenty-plus years I had kids in the house, I always kept the carpet clean. I fussed at the kids over the carpet, and everybody took off their shoes because of the carpet. Now I'd love to see more traffic and more mud and more apple juice on the carpet. I reached the goal, but the goal wasn't the most important goal."

When I was in high school, there was a guy whose goal was to have sex with as many girls as he could. It sounded like a good idea to him in high school. People told him he was the man. He was in control. He was smooth and popular and successful.

I saw him at my ten-year high school reunion.

He's already divorced, and he confessed to me his life feels empty.

He thought he was filling up, but really he was giving away pieces of himself he could never get back. He reached the goal, but reaching a goal is only as significant as the quality of the goal.

So if living happily ever after isn't the goal, what is? I believe the answer is illustrated in Jacob's life-altering encounter with the angel.

THE GOD OF JACOB

It had to have been the most dramatic moment in Jacob's overly dramatic life: "Your name will no longer be Jacob, but Israel" (Genesis 32:28).

Jacob must have thought God was saying, "Tired of who you are? Want to be somebody else? *Boom.* Wish granted. You have a new name and a new identity. You aren't weak, conniving, sneaky little Jacob anymore. You are Israel: a prince, a ruler, king of the mountain."

I'm sure Jacob was excited at the thought. He had spent his

life trying to be a self-made man. Now God himself was recognizing Jacob's achievement. It was the climax, the zenith, the magical moment of metamorphosis. Jacob was gone, and Israel was here to stay.

Only that's not what God meant at all.

We might expect that from this point forward the Bible would always refer to Jacob by his new name, Israel. But God has a funny way of ignoring our expectations. Usually it's to make a point.

Many years after this event God appeared to Moses in the burning bush. Exodus 3:15 describes how God told Moses that he wanted to be identified to the Israelites as the God of Abraham, the God of Isaac, and the God of . . .

Jacob.

Wait. Jacob?

Not Israel?

Israel was the new and improved Jacob, the triumphant and transformed Jacob. If you were God and wanted to make yourself known, wouldn't you call yourself the God of *Israel*? If you were launching a PR campaign to get your name out, wouldn't you want to be affiliated with the more positive side of this character?

Yet God said to Moses, and he says to us today, "If you want to know who I am, you need to understand I'm the God of Jacob too. I'm the God of all the mistakes you've made. I'm the God of all the parts of you that you don't want anybody to see. I'm not just the God of your success. I'm the God of your struggle. I'm not just the God of your victories. I'm the God of your defeats.

"I am
the God
of Jacob."

For the rest of his life and throughout the Bible, Jacob is called by both names. Sometimes he is called Jacob; sometimes he is called Israel. Why? Because we are complicated and so is change. Discovering who we are and who we are meant to become is a lifelong journey.

But in the meantime God isn't ashamed to be associated with Jacob, and he isn't ashamed to be associated with us, either.

Jacob's saga teaches us that life isn't about conquering our weaknesses so we can finally live happily ever after. It's about living *now,* just as we are, accepted by God and therefore able to accept ourselves.

It's about knowing that we are both Jacob and Israel at the same time. We are Jacob because we still struggle with stupid stuff. But we are Israel because God himself has spoken victory over us. True fulfillment is found in accepting both of those realities at the same time.

The more we can embrace them, the easier it becomes to reconcile them. That is, the more we understand that we are Israel in God's eyes, the less we will find ourselves acting like Jacob. Let's be honest. While we walk this planet, we'll never be fully free from our Jacob-like tendencies. But as long as we know that God has named us Israel, our habit of acting like Jacob can't hold us back. Our weaknesses, struggles, and mistakes will continually be converted into strengths through the power of God.

Win Within

In the Jacob narrative we see a man who fights with everyone. He wrestled Esau in the womb. He deceived his father into giving him a blessing that wasn't his. He sparred with his uncle Laban over everything, from his daughters to his donkeys. He tried to take down an angel and ended up lame.

Now Jacob was preparing to face his brother, Esau, again. It was decades down the road, and he was still struggling with the same thing.

Why? Because Esau wasn't the true opponent any more than the angel, his uncle, or his dad had been.

Jacob's outward struggles were the reflection of his inward struggles. He was a man in search of identity, transformation, and acceptance. And until he was able to find that in God, he could never be at rest with himself or the world around him.

The night he wrestled the angel, Jacob thought he was preparing to make peace with Esau. In reality, God brought him to that place to make peace with himself.

That was the point of the dual names. Jacob had to fight everything and everyone in a futile attempt to find his place in the world. Israel could rest in the acceptance of God.

The name Israel didn't imply perfection. It implied the purpose that God would bring forth through him. It implied the process of change. It implied relationship with the God who loved him as Jacob even as he was transforming him into Israel.

This is illustrated in Jacob's encounter with Esau a few verses and hours later. In comparison to his battle with the angel, the encounter was anticlimactic. Jacob planned to win the pardon of his brother by presenting him with elaborate gifts. But none of that turned out to be necessary.

When Jacob and Esau finally approached each other, the Bible says, "Esau ran to meet Jacob and embraced him; he threw his arms around his neck and kissed him. And they wept" (Genesis 33:4).

Standing face to face with the man he had spent his whole life struggling against, Jacob surely realized something I'm coming to understand more and more:

The only real battle I have to win is the one within.

The battle is not with Esau. The battle is with me.

Your real struggle is not with your money. Your real struggle is not with your employer. Your real struggle is not with your mother-in-law.

"You haven't met my mother-in-law," you might say.

Good point. But it's true nonetheless. The primary struggle you need to focus on is the struggle within.

I've met beautiful people who are insecure about the way they look. I've met people with eight-packs who talk about how fat they are. Acceptance, belonging, security, value, significance—the list goes on. We might manifest our needs differently, but we all desire the same things.

Perhaps one more Oprah reference will help us put this in perspective. I heard her say in a commencement address at Harvard University that the most important lesson she had learned in twenty-five years of talking to people was we all have this common denominator: we want to be validated; we want to be understood. She went on to say,

> I have done over 35,000 interviews in my career and as soon as that camera shuts off everyone always turns to me and inevitably in their own way asks this question "Was that okay?" I heard it from President Bush, I heard it from President Obama. I've heard it from heroes and from housewives. I've heard it from victims and perpetrators of crimes. I even heard it from Beyoncé in all her Beyoncéness. . . . [T]hey all want to know one thing: Was that okay?[17]

Only God (and occasionally Oprah) has the right to answer these questions:

Was that okay?

Am I okay?

And allowing him to answer these questions is the only way to win the war within our hearts. If we can defeat our internal insecurities, if we can embrace who we are and the process we are in, then it doesn't really matter what opposes us from without. We can overcome any struggle, any deficiency, any bank balance, any doctor's report, any enemy, any critic.

All we really have to do is win within.

Jacob's lifelong struggle culminated in the simple realization that life—with all its messiness, it's failures, and it's awkward moments—is meant to be lived in the light of God's acceptance. The goal of our existence is not perfection but relationship.

Jacob wasn't the only Bible hero who had to figure that out. If we fast-forward a couple of thousand years to the New Testament, we find that Peter and Paul both have something to teach us about reaching goals and finding fulfillment. They make an interesting contrast, actually, because the one you would expect to be closest to the goal ends up being the one further behind. Let me explain.

Throughout the Gospel narratives, Peter had a habit of leading with his mouth. I've mentioned this before. He loved to talk, and he was frequently wrong. Preachers like to poke fun at him, probably because most of us can relate to him. "Talking a lot" is at the top of our job description, after all.

The other day I was reading the story of the first miracle Peter performed after Jesus ascended into heaven. Peter and John went to the temple in Jerusalem to pray. There was a beggar outside who had been lame from birth. He asked Peter for money. Peter said, "Sorry, man, I don't have any change. Wish I did."

I'm sure the beggar heard that all day, every day. But then Peter added, "What I do have I give you. In the name of Jesus Christ of Nazareth, walk" (Acts 3:6). And the man did.

That created a lot of public chaos. Peter ended up preaching a powerful sermon to the crowd that gathered. The religious leaders responded by jailing Peter and John because they couldn't think of anything better to do. So Peter preached to them too. Then the Bible gives us this fascinating verse describing the religious leaders' reaction: "When they saw the courage of Peter and John and realized that they were unschooled, ordinary men, they were astonished and they took note that these men had been with Jesus" (4:13).

I love that. They were "unschooled, ordinary men." They didn't meet the qualifications of the religious leaders. They didn't live up to the expectations of their culture and society. In the eyes of their peers, they had nothing to say and no right to say it even if they did.

They were uniquely (un)qualified for the task of taking the gospel into the whole world.

But that didn't hold them back. They did miracles. They preached sermons. And Acts 4 records that while Peter and John were being hauled off to the local jail, two thousand more people joined the church.

The religious leaders were astonished by their confidence *despite their weakness.* And here's the kicker: that very incongruity was what led them to conclude that these men had been with Jesus.

Paul, on the other hand, was supremely qualified in the eyes of the Jewish leaders and people. Here is how he described his qualifications:

> If someone else thinks they have reasons to put confidence in the flesh, I have more: circumcised on the eighth day, of the people of Israel, of the tribe of Benjamin, a Hebrew of Hebrews; in regard to the law, a Pharisee; as for zeal, persecuting the church; as for righteousness based on the law, faultless. (Philippians 3:4–6)

Paul was incredible. He was the epitome of human achievement, the pinnacle of self-orchestrated perfection. Paul was the guy parents told their kids to be like when they grew up.

But Peter? He was just an ex-fisherman with a small budget and a big mouth. He didn't have what people thought he needed to represent God. He didn't have a résumé or a pedigree. He didn't have a master's degree in theology or a lineage worth bragging about. But because of what he *didn't* have, he reflected the one who was his goal to begin with.

To reach the #goals associated with being a good Jew, Peter would have needed to become more like Paul. But for the goals of the gospel to be accomplished, Paul actually had to become more like Peter. Paul had reached a lot of goals, but he had to let them go so he could look more like Jesus. He had to reject the things he used to think qualified him in order to achieve what was truly important. Paul continued his explanation:

> I consider everything a loss because of the surpassing worth of knowing Christ Jesus my Lord, for whose sake I have lost all things. I consider them garbage, that I may gain Christ and be found in him, not having a righteousness of my own that comes from the law, but that which is through faith in Christ—the righteousness that comes from God on the basis of faith. I want to know Christ. (verses 8–10)

What Paul had achieved wasn't wrong. But it wasn't the best goal. It wasn't worth spending his life on. Paul was saying, "Here's my goal now. I want to know Christ. I did all that other stuff. I saw all that other stuff. I had success that you couldn't imagine. I reached the goal, but when I got it, I found out I didn't want it. So I let go of that goal and got a new one: to know Jesus."

What is really interesting is that Paul wrote that from prison. Talk about a place of weakness. In the world's eyes he had fallen from grace. He had gone from Pharisee to prisoner, from respect to humiliation.

But for Paul, he was finally winning. Instead of qualifying himself, he was letting God qualify him. And the very things that other people might be embarrassed by were the things that propelled him into the destiny God had for him.

It gets even better. Verse 12 says, "Not that I have already obtained all this, or have already arrived at my goal, but I press on to take hold of that for which Christ Jesus took hold of me."

Paul's goals had changed. Impressing people, proving his worth, making it to the top—those things no longer held appeal. His life was now about knowing Jesus and becoming all that Jesus had called him to.

His life wasn't just about reaching a goal; it was about reaching for the goal. It was to "press on." It was to know Christ and to be found in him. It was to be qualified by God to accomplish the calling of God.

I believe the primary goal God has for us in this life is not that we would *arrive* but that we would *reach.* It is that we would, like Paul, be more focused on the journey of knowing Jesus and his will than on a destination. In a very real way, the journey is the destination and the process is the goal.

Of course, there are minidestinations along the way. And the ultimate destination is heaven. Once this life is over, we will have arrived at a place of complete relationship with God, complete holiness, and complete perfection.

But we aren't in heaven yet, friend. So if we make life about the way points, the viewpoints, and the high points instead of about the journey as a whole, we are going to miss out on much of what life has to offer.

By the way, when I say *reach,* I'm not talking about some frustrating, futile attempt to attain what we can never have. This isn't clutching at straws or grasping the wind. That wasn't Paul's attitude at all. *Pressing on* or *reaching* referred to the ongoing experience with God in this life that he knew would culminate in the next life. He was talking about the walk with God that had characterized all the great men and women of Scripture.

In the words of the English poet Robert Browning, "Ah, but a man's reach should exceed his grasp, or what's a heaven for?"[18]

Reaching implies process.

Reaching implies change.

Reaching implies relationship.

Reaching implies dependency.

In many ways the concept of reaching for Jesus, walking with Jesus, and knowing Jesus encapsulates everything I've been saying in this book.

Who qualifies us? And for what?

God qualifies us. For the journey and everything that entails.

The solution to being unqualified is to know Jesus. It's to enjoy the ups and downs and the ebbs and flows of life together with him. It's to face an uncertain future, not with the pride that comes from self-accomplishment or the fear that comes from self-loathing, but with the confidence that comes from having been with Jesus.

If you are a follower of Jesus, you already have everything you need to live a confident, fulfilled, productive life.

You can take off the masks and the armor. You can cease comparing and manipulating and pretending. You can stop trying to convince yourself that you are capable and competent in and of yourself.

Charge into the gap between who you are and all that God is calling you to become.

That's where growth happens.

And that's what grace is for.

A portion of the stained-glass window at
the Dora Maclellan Brown Memorial Chapel
Covenant College • Lookout Mountain, GA

Epilogue

Sometimes the creative process dispenses a little unexpected gift to affirm you're on the right track. This book went through three different titles and so many front-cover concepts I lost count. That's not abnormal or even noteworthy, but here's what *was* kind of weird.

After completely blowing the deadline, in sheer desperation I asked Ryan Hollingsworth, who has led the design team at our church for almost a decade, to mess around with a broken stained-glass motif. I told him that something featuring Moses would be ideal because he shows up early in the book. Most of all I wanted it to illustrate my favorite quote, the one by Leonard Cohen that appears at the front of the book, because it sums up the message: "There is a crack in everything. / That's how the light gets in."[19]

When I opened the e-mail with the cover as it appears now, I kind of knew, *Yeah, that's the one.*

But it wasn't until the next morning that I really knew. Not only that I had the right cover, but that I had written the right book.

When I asked Ryan to send me all the information he could

about the stained glass that inspired the artwork, first he told me the basics. It was a portion of a window in the chapel at Covenant College in Chattanooga, Tennessee.

And then he asked if I remembered speaking there around 2005 for a youth camp where he was a counselor. I didn't at first.

But later I did. And when I did, I remembered something else. That was the place where my wife, Holly, turned to me one night after I preached and said, "It's time for us to go start the church."

I argued with her for hours, listing all the reasons why I was unqualified. Too young, not good enough at administration, not even sure if I could come up with a new sermon every week—just to name a few.

I wish I could say that she delivered a zinger I've never forgotten and that a voice from heaven corroborated, saying, *This is your beloved wife, who is smarter than you. Listen to her.*

Instead, she listened patiently and looked at me like none of that mattered, because God had called me, and he was with me, and so was she. And I got the message.

About a year later our church was born.

Ten years later I still have my "why I'm unqualified" lists.

Moses had his list. So did Jacob. So do you.

But like the old preaching cliché says and like all who have trusted God have found along the way, God doesn't call the qualified. He qualifies the called.

I know it's just a book cover. But for me the circumstances surrounding it are a window through which I am reminded that God's ways are higher than mine.

And he still does big things through broken people.

ACKNOWLEDGMENTS

Thank you, Holly, for the gift of confidence. Thank you, Elijah, for changing my name. Thank you, Graham, for doing what must be done. Thank you, Abbey, for not letting the monsters come. Thank you, Mom, for putting words in me.

Justin Jaquith, it was a pleasure to partner with you. You went above and beyond to see this through. Thank you.

Chunks and Amy, you kept me going on this project, as you always do. Huey, your optimism and tenacity are the gold standard. Ryan, you're more talented than you even know. Jess, Christy, and Caroline, you are magicians.

Pastor Craig Groeschel, it's likely you wrote three books in the time it took me to write these acknowledgments. Thanks for a great example.

Alex, thanks for making sure this book happened.

Andrew, thanks for bringing such an optimistic outlook as you engaged with this message.

Carol, thank you for another thoughtful edit and for assassinating extraneous italics.

Thank you, Elevation Church, for supporting the calling of a pastor who has never felt qualified.

Dr. John MacArthur, thank you for the reminder.

NOTES

1. Bob Dylan, interview by Ed Bradley, "Dylan Looks Back," *60 Minutes,* CBS, December 5, 2004, www.cbsnews.com/news/dylan-looks-back/.
2. *Shrek,* directed by Andrew Adamson and Vicky Jenson (Universal City, CA: DreamWorks, 2001).
3. Cecilia Giménez, quote in Reuters, "Amateur Art Restorer Admits to Damaging Ecce Homo Mural—Video," *The Guardian,* August 22, 2012, www.theguardian.com/artanddesign/video/2012/aug/23/art-restorer-ecco-homo-mural-video. For other details see John Hall, "Elderly Woman Destroys 19th-Century Spanish Fresco by Elias Garcia Martinez in Botched Restoration," *The Independent,* August 22, 2012, www.independent.co.uk/arts-entertainment/art/news/elderly-woman-destroys-19thcentury-spanish-fresco-by-elias-garcia-martinez-in-botched-restoration-8073267.html.
4. Richard Rohr, *Following the Mystics through the Narrow Gate: Seeing God in All Things* (Albuquerque: Center for Action and Contemplation, 2010), CD-ROM.
5. A. W. Tozer, *The Knowledge of the Holy* (New York: HarperOne, 1978), 1.
6. J. I. Packer, *Knowing God* (Downers Grove, IL: InterVarsity, 1973), 19.
7. Gretchen Rubin, *Better Than Before: Mastering the Habits of Our Everyday Lives* (New York: Crown Publishers, 2015), 30.
8. Oswald Chambers, *My Utmost for His Highest* (Grand Rapids: Discovery House, 1992), April 19.

9. Prince, "Clouds," AZLyrics, www.azlyrics.com/lyrics/prince/clouds.html.
10. Axl Rose, "Breakdown," Guns N' Roses, *Use Your Illusion II,* Lyrics © Universal Music Publishing Group, 1991.
11. "Pinterest," *PC Magazine,* www.pcmag.com/encyclopedia/term/64546/pinterest.
12. C. S. Lewis, *Mere Christianity* (New York: Macmillan, 1960), 109.
13. "Lance Armstrong & Oprah Winfrey: Interview Transcript," January 18, 2013, BBC, www.bbc.com/sport/0/cycling/21065539.
14. "Lance Armstrong & Oprah Winfrey."
15. "Lance Armstrong & Oprah Winfrey."
16. Justine Harman, "The Problem with #Goals," *Elle,* www.elle.com/culture/tech/a27375/problem-with-goals-social-media/.
17. "Winfrey's Commencement Address: The Key to Life Is to Develop an Internal Moral, Emotional G.P.S.," May 31, 2013, *Harvard Gazette,* http://news.harvard.edu/gazette/story/2013/05/winfreys-commencement-address/.
18. Robert Browning, "Andrea del Sarto," www.poetryfoundation.org/poem/173001.
19. Shanna Crooks, Mike Strange, and Leonard Cohen, "Anthem," from *The Future,* Sony/ATV Songs LLC, Stranger Music Inc., 1992, www.azlyrics.com/lyrics/leonardcohen/anthem.html.